PARTNER *with* PURPOSE

D1553751

PARTNER *with* PURPOSE

Solving 21st Century Business Problems
Through Cross-Sector Collaboration

Steve Schmida

Founder of Resonance

Rivertowns
BOOKS

Copyright © 2020 by Steve Schmida. All rights reserved.

No part of this book may be used or reproduced by any means, graphic, electronic, or mechanical, including photocopying, recording, taping, or by any information storage retrieval system without the written permission of the publisher, except in the case of brief quotations embodied in critical articles and reviews.

Printed in the United States of America • March, 2020

Cloth edition: ISBN-13: 978-0-9790080-8-5
ISBN-10: 0-9790080-8-5

Paper edition: ISBN-13: 978-0-9790080-6-1
ISBN-10: 0-9790080-6-9

LCCN Imprint Name: Rivertowns Books

Rivertowns Books are available online from Amazon as well as from bookstores and other retailers. Requests for information and other correspondence may be addressed to:

Rivertowns Books
240 Locust Lane
Irvington NY 10533
Email: info@rivertownsbooks.com

Contents

To Naska—

May there never be a dull moment

Introduction:
The Smallholder Farmer and the Fortune 500 CEO

The life of a smallholder farmer in rural India seems a world away from the life of the CEO of one of the world's largest and most successful food and beverage companies. Farming in rural India has changed little in centuries. Most farmers tend small plots far from the bustling urban consumer markets of modern-day India, eking out a living with hours of backbreaking manual work in the fields. Farm productivity remains low, and rural communities are mired in poverty.

By contrast, the CEO of a Fortune 500 company is at the very pinnacle of international business. He or she travels the globe, attended by a coterie of advisors and staff. The CEO makes billion-dollar decisions on a nearly daily basis, under intense pressure from shareholders to deliver growth and profits while also facing new demands from consumers and employees alike—demands that the company should not only generate profit but also contribute to a better world.

Yet despite the vast differences between the life of a Fortune 500 CEO and an Indian farmer, the fates of the two are inextricably linked. Consider Ramon Laguarta, CEO of the multinational food and beverage company PepsiCo, a giant corporation with 230,000 employees and annual revenues of nearly $65 billion, and a farmer in the western Indian state of Gujarat, whom we'll call Aesha.

Aesha and her family supply potatoes to PepsiCo's Indian division. As one of the fastest growing markets in the world, India is of critical importance to the company's growth, which means it receives an outsized share of Ramon Laguarta's attention. Food and beverage markets in most Western countries are completely saturated. By contrast, India has a rapidly growing urban middle class, and demand for PepsiCo's snack foods is growing rapidly. Laguarta, therefore, is looking to fast-growing markets like India to drive revenue growth to meet the expectations of PepsiCo's shareholders. To meet the growing demand for PepsiCo products, the company needs to source ever more potatoes from smallholder farmers like Aesha in India and in other rapidly developing countries.

Unfortunately, agricultural production in India is not growing quickly enough to meet the rising demand. And increasing production is not a simple task. With a population of more than one billion, India is one of the world's most crowded regions, with little additional land available for cultivation. In addition, migration from the countryside to the cities is also shrinking the pool of agricultural workers and raising the average age of farmers. Among the workers who are available, many millions are women (like Aesha), a group that has historically been disempowered in Indian culture, which creates a range of social and economic problems for them when they seek to manage farms efficiently. Worse still, a changing climate with rising temperatures and increasingly erratic rainfall patterns is threatening to significantly lower the crop yields of farmers across India (and around the world). Importing large quantities of potatoes to meet the demand from India's burgeoning middle class would be expensive and could risk incurring the ire of India's government, which takes great pride in the country's ability to feed itself.

The more we examine these connections, the clearer it becomes that a Fortune 500 CEO's fate is very much tied to the ability of poor smallholder farmers like Aesha to deliver the commodities the company needs to fuel its growth strategy. We can start to see why increasing the productivity and the incomes of farmers in the company's supply chains is important to PepsiCo.

Solving the CEO's conundrum falls to Simon Lowden, Pepsico's chief sustainablity officer. Simon describes Pepsico's journey Pepsico this way: "As with many businesses today, we are making a transition from sustainability being a nice thing to do, run by passionate people, to operationalizing it and making sustainability into a real business driver."

PepsiCo's Sustainable Agriculture team is responsible for implementing Simon's vision through the PepsiCo Sustainable Farming Program. The team works across PepsiCo's myriad of global supply chains—responsible for sourcing potatoes, sugar cane, corn, chickpeas, and other materials—to align them with the company's commitment to "winning with purpose."

Margaret Henry and Rob Meyer are leaders in the Sustainable Agriculture team. Their goal is to increase PepsiCo's sourcing of agriculture produce to meet growing demand in a way that supports the sustainable growth of PepsiCo's brands and positively impacts the farmers in the company's supply chains.

Margaret and Rob see every day how the fates of PepsiCo and smallholder farmers around the world are interlinked, and how the ability of PepsiCo to grow and deliver value for share-holders increasingly depends on the company's ability to improve the lives and livelihoods of smallholder farmers across its vast global supply chains.

Margaret explains it very simply: "That farmer's livelihood is critical to our CEO's livelihood—because unless everyone wins, everyone loses."

Twenty-First Century Business— The Wicked New Normal

The existence of giant multinational corporations that rely on complex global supply chains is not a brand-new phenomenon. But today the logic of interdependence is more rigorous and demanding than ever.

For most of the 20th century, increasing the productivity and incomes of poor farmers in developing countries was largely the mission of governments and international bodies like the United Nations and the World Bank. Corporations focused mainly on a different array of challenges: increasing revenues and profitability, building market share, decreasing costs, and improving quality. The 20th century business professional pursued these goals using strategic and organizational tools like Six Sigma and Total Quality Management.

In the 21st century, however, companies are confronting a range of new kinds of business challenges. To explain what makes them different, let's start by differentiating three kinds of problems: *simple problems, complicated problems,* and *wicked problems.*

4

o Solving a simple problem can be compared to following the recipe for baking a cake. Although it may not be easy to bake a cake, if you follow the recipe and use the same ingredients and measurements every time, it should be possible to replicate the results consistently.

o A complicated problem requires a deeper level of expertise and experience. Consider what it takes to send a human being into space. The first time this was done, there were many unknowns and thousands of variables that had to be considered. Years of experimentation were required, and a number of fatalities were suffered because of the high levels of risk involved. But eventually, it became possible to send humans into space with relative safety and predictability by following a complex set of technical and managerial protocols, although it is still quite expensive and far from risk-free.

o There is *no* recipe or set of protocols you can use to solve a wicked problem. A wicked problem has economic, social, and environmental dimensions that interact with one another in ways that are ever-changing and unpredictable. As a result, many wicked problems are never completely solved. Instead, the best one can hope for is a process of continual improvement in addressing the issue.

One crucial characteristic of a wicked problem is that it is impossible for a single actor—whether a company, a government agency, or a community—to solve on its own. Today, business leaders in companies large and small are increasingly grappling with wicked problems they wouldn't have faced just a few decades ago.

As we've seen, PepsiCo's production managers are being asked to find ways to improve the consistency, quantity, and resilience of agricultural production in order to capitalize on enormous growth opportunities—even as climate change and other trends are negatively impacting crop yields. And this kind of wicked problem is not just a dilemma for PepsiCo. For companies in every business sector, wicked problems are becoming the new normal. Here are some typical examples:

- A professional charged with new market development at a leading tech company needs to find ways to expand the company's customer base in developing countries—where access to the Internet is inconsistent at best.

- A corporate sustainability executive with a leading seafood company is challenged with addressing the scourge of slavery in company supply chains.

- A biomedical engineer at a leading medical device company is charged with developing new lines of business to underserved health care markets in Africa and Asia, where access to health care services is hampered by poverty, lack of infrastructure, and other impediments.

- A business development manager at an African insurance company is looking for ways to expand into new, untested market segments at the so-called *base of the pyramid*, where millions of people have little or no experience with insurance.

6

o   A business association leader is charged with building
    a globe-spanning partnership of companies, govern-
    ments, and non-governmental organizations (NGOs)
    to promote the expansion of what's being called the
    circular economy as a means of reducing the human
    footprint on the planet.

Each of these business people has been asked to tackle a
problem that has never before been solved—a challenge with so
many economic, social, technical, and political complexities
that it's beyond the capacity of any one organization to address
successfully.

What's driving the emergence of such wicked problems for
companies? There are many factors. Here are a few of the most
important.

Changing consumer preferences. The Millennial generation—the largest in history—is driving a fundamental shift in
consumer behavior. We are now in the era of *conscious capitalism,* an age in which companies ignore the externalities of their
business models at their peril. Customers want to know that the
brands they are consuming are aligned with their environmental
and social value. This isn't just fluff and rhetoric—it is a bottom-
line issue, as reflected in its financial impact. For example, according to a 2017 study, companies that are more sustainable
outperform their less-sustainable counterparts by 40 percent.

Demand for corporate purpose. There is a growing body of
evidence that companies that have a clear purpose beyond profitability attract and retain better employees and achieve better
results. For example, a 2019 study described in the *Harvard Business Review* found that those companies that put their purpose
at the core of their strategies achieved better financial results

and enjoyed enhanced greater employee retention and engagement. Thus, companies cannot expect to attract the best talent if they are perceived as harming the communities in which they operate and other stakeholders—which means that companies are required to embrace tough challenges that go far beyond simply making money.

Social license to operate. In a growing number of industries, companies are faced with having to win acceptance of their business practices and operations from outside stakeholders, including regulatory agencies, community organizations, and civic associations. If they lack this social license to operate, companies may experience intense pressure from media criticism, lawsuits, protest campaigns, consumer boycotts, and other attacks. Companies in industries like mining, oil and gas, tobacco, and firearms have faced such pressures for decades, but today many other industries, from agriculture to high technology, are facing them, too.

Climate change and resource depletion. As Larry Fink, the CEO of BlackRock, Inc. has highlighted, companies and investors can no longer afford to ignore the impact of climate change on their supply chains as well as the markets they serve. Investors are starting to demand that companies address climate change risks in their operations and supply chains. At the same time, the depletion of natural resources is forcing companies to do more with less.

The rise of the rest. Until recently, companies could enjoy solid growth in sales and profitability by focusing solely on the familiar developed markets of North America, Europe, and Japan. Today the whole world is being transformed into a potential market. In 2018, for the first time in human history, more than half the world's population was in the middle class—a stunning development. This *rise of the rest* across Africa, Latin America, and the less-developed parts of Asia creates huge market opportunities for companies able to develop products and services that these emerging consumers need and want—as well as huge challenges for multinational and local companies alike.

These issues are impacting industries in different ways and at varying levels of intensity, but none of them are likely to go away anytime soon—which means that businesses large and small need to develop strategies for dealing with them.

Twentieth century business tools will not solve these new types of wicked problems. They are simply too multifaceted for any company to solve on its own. As PepsiCo's Rob Meyers notes, "To solve some of these systemic issues in our supply chain that we have found in implementing our Sustainable Agriculture Program is something we can't do on our own. Even if we could just write a check, we couldn't write one big enough to fix these systemic issues." The new normal of wicked 21st century business problems requires different tools.

The Cross-Sector Partnership: A Vital Tool for 21st Century Business

Tackling wicked business problems requires a new approach: one in which companies engage and partner with other actors—governments, charitable foundations, NGOs, universities, think tanks, faith-based groups, civic associations, and more—in ways that create both business value and lasting social and environmental benefits. The resulting *cross-sector partnerships* are emerging as a critical tool for companies faced with wicked 21st century business problems.

Cross-sector partnerships are not entirely new, but they are growing in prominence and popularity as companies, governments, and NGOs butt up against complicated and wicked problems that resist simple solutions. And as cross-sector partnerships become more mainstream, they are placing new demands on professionals. Working across sectors is not a natural instinct or skill for most business professionals. The needs, incentives, cultures, and timelines of governments, nonprofits, and philanthropic organizations are fundamentally different from those of most businesses.

This is a point PepsiCo's Rob Meyers knows all too well. "When you have a businessperson and a donor representative together for the first time, they are talking different languages," Rob says. "What's important to the donor and the business seem different, so it seems as if it might be impossible for them to work together." To overcome the challenges of communicating and collaborating across sectors, business professionals need to learn new skills and employ new tools.

That is what *Partner with Purpose* is all about. In its pages, we'll look at cross-sector partnerships from the perspective of the business professional who is seeking ways to solve wicked problems in the era of conscious capitalism. It is a hands-on guide for busy people looking to *get things done* and achieve positive impact through partnerships.

Of course, leaders from government, academia, and the NGO community are also key players in cross-sector partnerships, and their perspectives are critically important. Fortunately, these individuals can turn to a number of excellent resources and publications from organizations like the Intersector Project, the Partnering Initiative, and the PPPLab, which provide a rich understanding of partnerships from the perspectives of civil society and government. Other fine sources include the books *Social Value Investing: A Management Framework for Effective Partnerships* by Howard Buffett and William Eimike (Columbia University Press, 2018) and *Creating Value in Nonprofit-Business Collaborations* by James E. Austin and M. May Seitanidi (Jossey-Bass, 2014). *The Annual Review of Social Partnerships* offers additional valuable insights. Rather than duplicate these kinds of resources, *Partner with Purpose* seeks to complement them by presenting partnerships in a new way that is grounded in the realities of 21st century business.

This book is divided into two major sections. Chapters one through four give an overview of cross-sector partnerships, the problems they solve, what they look like, and why they matter. Chapters five through eleven offer tactical recommendations on how to build and manage partnerships, how to measure their results, and how to build an effective partnership team. While the concepts in the book build upon one another, each chapter is self-contained, so that busy professionals in need of specific guidance can flip to the relevant chapter and quickly find what they need.

Each chapter tackles a specific component of cross-sector partnerships and is informed by the experience of talented business professionals from an array of industries, including technology, food and beverage, insurance, and health care, and a wide range of companies, from familiar companies and brands like Medtronic, Microsoft, and PepsiCo to dynamic emerging market companies like Thai Union in Thailand and miLife Insurance in Ghana. Through the stories of dedicated business professionals at companies like these, we will explore how cross-sector partnerships can achieve lasting impact and build business value.

As you learn about partnerships, you will also embark on a journey across frontier markets in Africa, Asia, Latin America, and beyond. We will go from the C-suites of some of the world's leading companies to rural villages in Sri Lanka, from the oil fields of the Caspian Sea to fishing communities in Ghana, to see how companies are partnering with NGOs, donors, governments, and communities to create business value while driving positive social and environmental impacts.

Partner with Purpose is also shaped and enriched by the work of the company I founded, Resonance, which specializes in fostering cross-sector partnerships to solve wicked business problems around the world. Our team of more than 100 Resonators helps clients tackle problems ranging from climate change to human trafficking to supply chain sustainability. We have seen what works and what does not in cross-sector collaboration. In particular, our Learn, Align, Build, Scale/Sustain (LABS) methodology is informed by our work with clients in more than 80 countries. This book is a testament to the commitment of our clients in tackling some of the great challenges of our age.

If you are a business professional who is new to cross-sector partnerships, you will find *Partner with Purpose* a useful primer. If you are already an experienced partnership pro, it will provide useful tips, tools, and stories that will help you further strengthen your skills as you work to solve the wicked business problems of the 21st century.

Let's get started.

1

Cross-Sector Partnerships and Why They Matter

- o What is a cross-sector partnership?
- o How cross-sector partnerships differ from other business partnerships
- o What constitutes an effective cross-sector partnership?
- o The kinds of wicked business problems that cross-sector partnerships can address

Dateline: Kazakhstan. The beginning of my cross-sector partnership journey was pure happenstance. In the late 1990s, my wife and I were living in Almaty, Kazakhstan, where I was the regional director for an American NGO called the Eurasia Foundation (EF). Officials from the George H. W. Bush and Clinton administrations had set up the Eurasia Foundation to provide government-supported grants to local organizations in the newly independent states of the former Soviet Union. I was in charge of programs in Kazakhstan and Kyrgyzstan—two new countries in Central Asia. In this role, I was charged with giving out small grants to support local organizations to help foster entrepreneurship, improve education, and strengthen nascent civil society.

For me, a 25-year-old who had graduated from college with a degree in Russian studies and few employment prospects, this was a remarkable opportunity. I was living in Central Asia and supporting local civic leaders and entrepreneurs during truly historic times. I had a budget of three million dollars and a staff of 30 gifted local professionals. Perhaps best of all, my boss was 7,000 miles away in Washington!

To say I was in over my head was something of an understatement. I had no previous management experience or training. Though I had lived in Central Asia previously (two years in Kyrgyzstan), I was far from an expert. Luckily for me, in the 1990s, American speakers of Russian who had some knowledge of Central Asia were something of a rare commodity. In addition, I had an "extradictable passport," which means that, in the event that the foundation's funds were stolen or misused—a not-insignificant risk in some of the most corrupt countries in the world—I could be hauled back to the United States for prosecution. This was an important qualification for a employee who would be doling out U.S. taxpayer funds. Those bare minimum qualifications were enough to get me the job.

These were heady, tumultuous days across the region. Kazakhstan and Kyrgyzstan had no modern history as independent states. They'd become sovereign countries overnight following the collapse of the Soviet regime in August, 1991. It is hard to imagine just how much of a shock this was to the people and institutions living in the newly-formed countries. Imagine if U.S. states the size of Minnesota and New York suddenly found themselves independent countries. Everything had to be created from scratch: government ministries, currencies, diplomatic relations. It was a chaotic, exciting time.

What's more, the collapse of the Soviet Union was not only a political earthquake. It also precipitated the largest single economic decline in recorded history. As the communist command economy gave way to a new market-based system in the period from 1990 to 1999, real GDP declined by more than 40 percent across the region. Living standards plummeted as inefficient Soviet-era factories closed and new privately owned businesses struggled to emerge. Meanwhile, corruption across the region exploded as government officials cashed in on the sale of state assets. In the year 2000, Kazakhstan was ranked one of the most corrupt countries in the world, on a par with Robert Mugabe's Zimbabwe.

Despite all these problems—or perhaps because of them—I considered my assignment at EF to be a dream job. I had a ringside seat to history in the making, supporting civic leaders, activists, and entrepreneurs as they worked to build new societies virtually overnight.

I was a bit surprised one day in early 2000 when Ed Verona, the head of Texaco for Kazakhstan, invited me to his offices in one of the swank new five-star hotels in Almaty, the largest city in Kazakhstan. At the time, it was pretty unusual for an American oil company executive to invite the head of an NGO to their office. Generally speaking, oil companies and NGOs were quite wary of each other, since the two groups had often clashed regarding oil industry environmental and governance practices. To be honest, I did not know what to expect.

Ed was a savvy former U.S. foreign service officer with a deep understanding of the realities of the region. Having served in the U.S. embassy in Moscow and boasting a fluent knowledge of Russian, he had a very good handle on the political realities Texaco faced in the regional oil sector. Now he laid out for me the challenge the company was facing.

Like many western oil companies at the time, Texaco was jockeying to obtain access to the newly available oil fields in the Caspian basin in Western Kazakhstan. The company was currently eyeing a major new field in the region surrounding Aktau, a port city on the eastern shores of the Caspian Sea. Because of the myriad of permits required by local agencies, the company was eager to develop and maintain strong relationships with officials at the city, *oblast* (provincial), and national levels.

Now, however, Texaco was coming under pressure from the governor of Aktau to make a major financial contribution to the refurbishment of a local sports stadium. But when Texaco staff visited the stadium, they discovered that most of the renovations had already been completed. They realized that any funds from

Texaco would likely wind up lining the pockets of local officials. This would create both a reputational and legal risk, since it could cause the company to run afoul of the Foreign Corrupt Practices Act (FCPA), a U.S. law that imposes strict penalties for corrupt acts by Americans and American firms.

For all these reasons, Ed told me that Texaco did not want any part of a scheme that enriched a government official. But as long as the company remained passive, it would face pressure from local officials. If they became upset with Texaco, they could easily throw up administrative and bureaucratic barriers that would make it impossible for the company to work in the country. "We need to be proactive," Ed said. "We have to demonstrate how Texaco can benefit the local community in a transparent, responsible manner, and do so in a way that also makes the governor look good."

What's more, there was growing time pressure on Texaco. Later that same year, senior executives from across the oil industry would descend on Kazakhstan to celebrate the centennial of the industry in the country. It was expected and hoped that Texaco might use the occasion to highlight its leadership in reviving Kazakhstan's oil industry.

Ed had called on me because of EF's reputation for transparency and accountability as well as its credibility with government officials at both the national and local levels. "Do you have any ideas for impactful projects that Texaco can support in the Aktau region?" he asked. "If so, is there any way we can support those projects with help from the foundation?"

From EF's perspective, the idea of a collaboration made sense. We were looking to expand our program footprint deeper into Western Kazakhstan, and we recognized that the oil industry was going to be central to the future economy there. When I took the opportunity back to my team members at the EF office, most of them were excited. At the time, EF was exploring a possible project with Caspian State University in Aktau to create a law library and an Internet center. Access to information in remote communities like Aktau was very limited. A law library would give promising students access to modern textbooks, The expanded facilities, including new equipment, textbooks, and teacher training, would be used to prepare young professionals to work in the country's re-emergent oil industry. At the same time, the proposed Internet center (sometimes referred to as a *telecenter*) would provide a much-needed digital window on the wider world. This was a project that aligned very well with Texaco's needs and would have a significant positive impact on the lives of young students and professionals in Aktau.

"It was a perfect coincidence," as Ed would later recall. We agreed to launch a collaborative effort that would benefit all the involved stakeholders.

The next couple of months were a whirlwind of negotiations and preparations. We had to figure out how our partnership would work. We had to develop some sort of agreement that would define the roles of the partners, both financially and in terms of activities and programs. We had to sort out how key decisions were going to be made and by whom—the local university, EF, Texaco? EF also had to work intensively with the university officials to ensure that they were ready to receive and manage the funds appropriately. I flew a team of grant managers out to Aktau to work with the university administration to train them on our financial reporting requirements.

I also had some internal coalition-building to do within EF. While most of our Kazakhstani staff were highly supportive of the partnership, a few were skeptical about working with a company from the oil sector, an industry whose historical environmental practices left much to be desired. We had several internal meetings to discuss the joint effort with Texaco, including at least one where we invited the head of a local environmental NGO to participate. Gradually, those discussions enabled us to reach the level of buy-in we needed in order to move forward.

Meanwhile, on the Texaco side, Ed felt growing pressure to show results in advance of the Kazakhstan's oil industry's centennial. "We needed to move quickly," says Ed. And this required overcoming some internal resistance within Texaco. Ed focused his arguments on the benefits the company would receive in terms of improved social license to operate. The law library and Internet center project would give Texaco a degree of credibility and a reputational boost that would help make the company a respected part of the regional business community. In addition, by working with EF and the university, the company would avoid any appearance of impropriety.

Within a few months, I found myself in Aktau for the launch of the program during the oil industry's centennial celebration. Founded in the 1950s as a center for the mining and processing of uranium, Aktau was a dusty port city of 190,000 that was still reeling from the collapse of the Soviet Union eight years earlier. Many of the buildings on Aktau's waterfront seemed to be practically tumbling over into the Caspian.

Ed, his boss from Texaco headquarters, the governor of the *oblast*, the rector of Caspian State University, and a number of other local dignitaries attended the launch event. Smiling for photographers from the local press, the governor cut the ribbon officially opening the Internet center and the law library. It marked the launch of a partnership that would prove to be a big success for Texaco, EF, the university, and most important, the local students.

"The partnership took huge pressure off us," Ed recalls. "The governor was happy, and we had done something that would benefit the local community. The association with the Eurasia Foundation was beneficial, too, because it showed that we were committed to transparency. Suddenly, Texaco was the top western oil company in Aktau."

There were also benefits for EF. A company-NGO partnership was quite a novelty in 2000, and suddenly other companies and funders were eager to work with EF. What's more, we had shown that there were ways that Western companies could build and maintain their social license to operate without bribing local officials even in a place as corrupt as Kazakhstan.

Like so many in the chaotic years following the collapse of the Soviet Union, Ed and I were merely improvising to make something good happen in an uncertain and rapidly evolving environment. We did not realize we were launching what would now be more commonly known as a cross-sector partnership. We were simply joining forces to address our complementary needs and goals. Texaco needed EF's knowledge of the Kazakh education system and our skills with transparent financial management. EF was glad to access additional outside funds that enabled us to expand the reach of our programs. Caspian State University benefitted from enhanced resources that would improve their ability to prepare students for careers in the burgeoning oil industry in Kazakhstan.

As for me, I would go on to fund public access Internet centers at libraries, universities, and NGOs across Central Asia. And while I didn't know it at the time, the concept of cross-sector collaboration would form a central part of my professional journey over the next two decades.

What is a Cross-Sector Partnership?

While the Texaco-EF partnership was relatively novel at the turn of the century, cross-sector partnerships are now much more commonplace. Companies ranging from Starbucks to Bechtel are working collaboratively with NGOs, donors, governments, and other types of organization to address a wide range of social, economic, and environmental issues impacting their businesses, from eliminating human trafficking in supply chains in Asia to increasing access to HIV/AIDS medicines in Africa.

Partnerships, of course, are nothing new. The business world employs many types of partnerships. Law firms and other types of professional service firms are typically organized as limited liability partnerships (LLPs). Companies themselves often form what are called *precompetitive alliances*, such as the partnership between Honda and GM to develop new battery technologies to power tomorrow's electric vehicles. Governments often outsource infrastructure projects and other services to the private sector. The resulting public-private partnerships—the well-known Dulles Toll Road in the suburbs of Washington, D.C., for example—are an important tool for facilitating investment in roads and airports as well as public services like sanitation.

All of these types of partnerships are important tools for business and government that have been well documented and understood for many decades. The focus of this book is on partnerships that work across sectors—industry, nonprofit, and government—to achieve shared goals. Howard Buffett and William

Eimicke of Columbia University define a cross-sector partnership as "a voluntary collaboration between two or more organizations from two or more sectors that leverage their respective teams and resources to achieve mutually agreed-upon and measurable goals." Harvard Business School's Michael Porter and Mark Kramer coined the term *shared value* to describe the results of these collaborations. In these cross-sector partnerships, the relationship is not hierarchical. Rather, the parties must collaborate, invest resources together, and share roles and responsibilities in pursuit of a shared vision of success.

Ed Martin, a former branding and marketing executive with companies such as Ford, Kellogg's, and Coca-Cola, is the co-founder of 5th Element Group, a consulting firm that specializes in cross-sector partnerships. Martin calls these cross-sector partnerships *omniwins*, because they enable business, government, and society as a whole to benefit. "Everyone who comes together needs to be lifted and so does the world," says Martin, and he adds, "These *omniwins* enable brands to connect more deeply and authentically with today's consumers." Martin and his team are so committed to the term that his current title with the company is Chief Omniwin Officer.

Whether they are described using the terms cross-sector partnerships, public-private partnerships, shared value, or omniwins, these collaborations have garnered a great deal of attention in recent years. However, they are generally poorly understood, especially in the business community, since much of the writing about them has been designed for academic, public-sector, and nonprofit audiences.

Why Do Cross-Sector Partnerships Matter?

Let's go back to the Texaco example. The problem that the company was facing was complicated. There was significant political pressure from the Kazakhstani government to "do something" in an economically depressed part of the country. The local government was pushing the company to invest in a white-elephant project that had a strong whiff of corruption about it—something Texaco executives and shareholders saw as a significant potential financial and legal liability. As a result, Texaco found that its cost of operations was under pressure while its social license to operate and its reputation were at risk. Texaco's leaders had basically three options.

1. *Do nothing.* Texaco could have tried to simply pretend the problem did not exist, but this would have done little to solve the underlying issues. The company would have risked incurring the ire of the Kazakhstani government even while preparing to bid on future oil concessions. Doing nothing would not have improved the company's cost of operations, nor would it have alleviated the pressure from the local government o support its stadium project.

2. *Go it alone.* Texaco could have tried to tackle this problem on its own—for example, by researching, selecting, designing, and implementing a local social project to benefit the Kazakhstan community without help from any outside organization. The company had plenty of very bright professionals it could have assigned to these tasks. However, while Texaco is very skilled at pulling oil out of the ground and

getting it to market—its core competency—establishing effective social programs is another matter. Therefore, going it alone would involve significant execution risk for Texaco as well as the risk of inadvertently becoming entangled in actual or perceived corruption.

3. *Partner with organizations that share Texaco's goals, but have more germane core competencies and capabilities.* This is the option Texaco chose. By partnering with EF, Texaco benefited in three ways. EF brought expertise and credibility in higher education to reduce the execution risk associated with the project; it brought a high level of financial transparency to reduce the risk of corruption; and its positive reputation with key stakeholders in both the central and local governments gave Texaco and the project an instant credibility that would have otherwise been unattainable.

When we look at the company's options this way, the decision to forge a partnership is glaringly obvious. This gets to the heart of why cross-sector partnerships matter: They enable companies to tackle complicated, wicked problems that they cannot solve on their own.

From this point onward in the book, I will often refer to cross-sector partnerships simply as *partnerships*. Such partnerships serve as the major focus of Resonance, the consulting firm I founded and where I serve as chief innovation officer. Through our work on more than 300 cross-sector collaborations, we've defined several key objectives that every effective partnership should embrace.

- *Develop common goals.* When developing a partnership, each organization's goals should be taken into consideration and incorporated into the overall goals of the partnership. But thereafter, the overall goals of the partnership should be recognized and treated as more important than the goals of any one organization in the partnership.
- *Create a framework of shared risks and rewards.* Each partner needs to understand the perspectives, success metrics, and assets of the other partners, and should be incentivized to achieve the same objectives.
- *Leverage the resources and capabilities of the partners.* An effective partnership is about leveraging the unique resources and capabilities of the partners—not just funding but also access to markets, domain expertise, networks, convening authority, and so on.
- *Build sustainable innovations.* When partnerships focus on short-term rather than long-term goals, it can produce the sense that "Everything is a pilot project." To avoid this result, it's important to build a common understanding of long-term goals and to build in mechanisms that allow partnerships to continue to thrive over time. In the context of a cross-sector partnership, *sustainability* means the ability of the positive results generated by a partnership to persist without ongoing support from the partners.
- *Be sensitive to the complexity of local communities.* Every geographic region has its unique dynamics, political structures, languages, cultures, and types of partners. A good partnership should build on the

knowledge and expertise of staff and organizations on the ground who understand the local context.

o *Measure results.* As all smart business people know, what gets measured gets done. Strong partnerships measure their progress toward clearly defined results, enabling the partners to make smart, informed decisions about what is working and what is not.

When companies incorporate these characteristics into the partnerships they build, they are far more likely to achieve the results they are looking for.

Wicked Business Problems That Partnerships Can Address

Companies today are facing a growing number of wicked problems, particularly in frontier and emerging markets in Africa, Asia, and Latin America. Here are some of the most common problem areas where businesses are forging partnerships with international organizations, NGOs, civil society groups, donor agencies, host governments, and other types of partners.

Supply chain sustainability. Many companies face growing challenges to the safety and sustainability of their supply chains, from PepsiCo looking to increase the supply of potatoes from smallholder farmers in India to Thai Union seeking to eliminate human slavery aboard the ships that supply its seafood (an example we'll explore in a later chapter).

New market development. As markets in developed economies become saturated, companies are looking increasingly to explore market opportunities among lower-income countries and base-of-the-pyramid consumers. However, accessing these markets is complex and often requires non-traditional business models and modalities—including cross-sector partnerships.

Workforce development. Companies face increasing challenges in accessing healthy and skilled workers, particularly in countries where the formal education system may be inadequate to meet the needs of a knowledge-based 21st century workforce.

Climate change and sustainability. As the impacts of climate change become increasingly acute, companies face major challenges in improving the sustainability of their operations and the operations of their suppliers and vendors.

Social license to operate. As companies as varied as rideshare app Uber and global mine operator Rio Tinto have found to their peril, losing social license to operate in a market can be very costly. The rise of social media means that news about an isolated problem in a single location can go viral in a matter of hours.

If you are business professional, you already know how truly complex these kinds of challenges can be. Your company cannot simply develop a new technology or buy a piece of software to solve these problems, nor can you hire a PR firm to make them disappear. These challenges are often simply too multifaceted for your company to tackle on its own. Which is why these are the types of problems that partnerships were meant to solve. Partnerships help companies tackle these problems by bringing the resources, expertise, and legitimacy of donor agencies, governments, and NGOs to bear on the problem at hand. At their best, partnerships enable companies to address wicked problems by tackling them from a variety of angles simultaneously to achieve better results, as summarized in Figure 1-1.

Figure 1-1: Partnerships Can Achieve Better Results

Increased Scale	• Reach more people in more places • Amplify outcomes • Expand impact and results • Leverage outside resources
Replicability and Sustainability	• Spark continued investment • Increase opportunities for long-term investments • Create models that can be widely adapted
Improved Effectiveness	• Introduce new collaboration methods • Innovate through shared expertise • Build the capacities of all stakeholders • Unlock new funding streams and opportunities
Better Efficiency	• Achieve coordinated change and impact • Reach long-term goals more quickly • Require smaller funding commitments • Reduce need to repeat interventions
Systemic Change	• Make fundamental changes in the way the world works • Cultivate new leadership approaches and organizational strategies for businesses, NGOs, governments

For Ed Verona and Texaco, the partnership we forged helped his team solve a major problem the company was facing in its operations in Kazakhstan. As it happened, unbeknownst to any of us at the time, just a few months later, industry rival Chevron would acquire Texaco in what was then the largest oil industry merger in history. Our partnership ensured that Texaco's operations in Western Kazakhstan would not become a bone of contention during the merger.

More important, the partnership helped lay the foundation for modern business and management education in Western Kazakhstan, opening career and life opportunities for promising students in a remote but economically important part of the world.

As for me, I found the whole experience fascinating. I got to learn a fair bit about the oil industry, whose challenges and opportunities were so different from the ones I faced in my work in the nonprofit world. I also enjoyed my first glimpse of the power of bringing together organizations across sectors to solve big, important societal challenges.

In short, I was hooked on cross-sector partnerships and their potential to help change the world.

2

To Partner or Not? Questions You Need to Ask

- The types of business problems that cross-sector partnerships are made to address
- Questions to ask when you're considering whether a partnership is the right step for you
- Five good reasons *not* to partner

Dateline: Thailand. One of the world's most important industries is also one of its most troubled: seafood. The source of more than 20 percent of the world's protein, seafood consumption is expected to grow rapidly in coming decades.

The problem is that, while demand for seafood is increasing, global fish stocks are being depleted at a stunning pace. According to the Food and Agriculture Organization of the United Nations (FAO), fully 90 percent of commercial fish stocks are either currently fully fished or overfished. What's worse, the seafood industry is rife with social and environmental problems: forced labor and slavery, unsafe work conditions, and illegal, unregulated, and unreported fishing. Newer forms of seafood production, such as aquaculture, also bring a host of labor and environmental issues.

Few people know these problems better than Darian McBain. Darian is global director for sustainability and corporate affairs at Thai Union. Founded by the Chansiri family, among the wealthiest in Thailand, Thai Union is one of the world's largest seafood processors, with brands such as Chicken of the Sea in the United States and John West in the United Kingdom. A trained engineer with a diverse professional background in environmental sustainability and public health with organizations as diverse as the World Wildlife Federation and Britain's National Health Service, Darian joined Thai Union in 2015. Shortly before, the Thai seafood industry had been excoriated in the *Guardian* and the *New York Times* over the widespread prevalence of slavery aboard ships and at processing facilities in Asia. In addition, Greenpeace and many environmental activists were aggressively attacking the company in the press and in social media.

Darian was joining a company in crisis. "Everybody hated us," she recalls. "We were considered the worst in the world."

At the time, Thai Union had only a small two-person team dedicated to corporate social responsibility (CSR), primarily focused on funding charities in Thailand. But, in any case, the challenges facing the company were far more complex than those that could be addressed through a traditional CSR program. In the wake of the damaging news coverage, the European Union (EU) slapped the Thai seafood industry with a "yellow card"—a warning that, if it did not clean up its act and improve regulation of the fisheries sector, Thai-sourced seafood would be banned from the EU, one of the world's largest seafood markets.

Solving the company's problems would not be simple. Thai Union did not own, control, operate, or have full visibility over many of the vessels in its supply chain, which operated far out at sea, beyond the reach of outside monitors. There is no formula or recipe for dealing with human slavery at sea, and stopping illegal fishing in far-flung oceans across a variety of legal jurisdictions is immensely difficult. No single company—even an industry leader like Thai Union—could solve such problems on its own.

Moreover, the company, like the industry as a whole, faced tremendous cost pressures. Seafood is largely a commodity product, meaning it is purchased in bulk with low price being a key factor in purchasing choices. This meant that any increase in costs to fix the problems would almost certainly come straight out of the company's bottom line. Yet a failure to solve them could put the company's future at risk.

Considering a Partnership?
Start by Defining Your Problem

Given the breadth and complexity of the problems faced by Thai Union, it was natural for the company's leaders to want to explore the possibility of working with other organizations to address them—in other words, the creation of a cross-sector partnership. But how to begin?

When a company is considering the partnership option, there are three key questions to answer.

- *What is the problem we are trying to solve?* Getting clear on the problem to be solved is a critical first step in determining whether a cross-sector partnership might be the right tool. In this context, the term *problem* may mean more than a headache or a challenge; a problem can also refer to a business or market opportunity. For example, in a later chapter, you'll meet Terry Amartei from Ghana's miLife Insurance company, who faced the problem of insuring workers from Ghana's vast informal sector—a challenge that was also a major business opportunity for his company and the other partners.

- *Is the problem simple, complicated, or wicked?* Cross-sector partnerships are time-consuming to build and manage. Therefore, partnerships are generally recommended only for addressing complicated and wicked problems that no single company or organization can tackle independently.

○ *Are there other organizations that are facing the same problem and share your need to solve it?* This last question is critical. Partnerships depend on having partners who share a problem in common. If your problem is strictly internal or unique to your company, outside organizations are not going to be interested in partnering with you to solve it. (Some may be interested in having you pay them to solve it, but this is a vendor relationship, not a partnership).

Let's examine how Daria McBain and her team at Thai Union tackled this three-step process.

Analyzing the Problem

The first step for considering the possibility of a cross-sector partnership is to get very clear on the problem to be solved or, as Harvard's Clayton Christensen puts it, "the job to be done." What is your company trying to achieve? Are you trying to capitalize on a new opportunity, mitigate a future risk, or address an ongoing challenge? Is the problem you face a simple, complicated, or wicked one?

Cross-sector partnerships are time-consuming to build and manage, so they are not terribly efficient or effective at solving *simple* problems. As David McGinty, global director of the Platform for Accelerating the Circular Economy (PACE) says, "If you can do it on your own, do it." That will almost always be the easiest and most expedient way to address a simple problem.

However, if the problem you face is complicated or, heaven help you, wicked, then partnership may be a tool worth considering. Partnerships are a powerful tool for solving complicated and wicked problems because they enable companies to engage organizations and institutions that possess resources, capabilities, and expertise that private-sector companies lack.

Darian and her small sustainability team started by defining the problems they faced. They quickly realized that Thai Union faced three overlapping wicked problems—challenges that had little chance of being fixed unless Darian's team could identify and work with partners who had the capabilities and resources to help them tackle the different facets of the problems.

Labor conditions on vessels and in facilities. The exposure of unethical labor practices on board fishing vessels and at processing facilities posed a truly wicked problem for Thai Union. Seafood supply chains are enormously complex. It's not unusual for the fish on your plate to be caught and landed in the Western Pacific, landed in Vanuatu, processed in Thailand, and then imported to the United States. This long, winding product journey makes it difficult for company managers to get visibility on what is happening in the supply chain. What's more, much of the labor in the seafood industry is migrant labor, largely from low-income Mekong River countries like Cambodia, Burma, and Laos, creating huge language and cultural barriers as well as presenting challenges for jurisdiction. Finally, it's very difficult and expensive to provide on-vessel monitoring or communications for workers or boats at sea.

Unsustainable fishing practices. With socially and environmentally-conscious consumers demanding more sustainable products in markets in the European Union and the United States, unsustainable fishing practices presented a major brand-reputation problem—especially for Thai Union, with its numerous consumer-facing brands. But transforming the traditional fishing methods used by the supplier fleets would be a complicated and expensive proposition.

Legal and regulatory compliance. Bad publicity meant that Thai Union faced intense pressure from NGOs and the media. In response, governments in Europe and North America were putting in place new, much stricter regulations regarding the import of seafood to ensure sustainability as well as *traceability,* that is, the ability to track a seafood product "from bait to plate." These new rules would raise the bar on Thai Union's social license to operate as well as hiking the company's costs.

With the problems well defined, Darian convinced Thai Union's leadership that there was no way the company could address them on their own. Fortunately, Darian found that Thai Union's executives and the Chansiri family were equally appalled by the problems and shared her desire to resolve them. "Thai Union is a business with a family at heart," she says, "and we had tremendous support—not just for purely business reasons, but also for moral and ethical reasons."

Identifying Potential Partners

With company leadership on board, Darian could focus her efforts on identifying and engaging potential partners who had resources, expertise, or capabilities for addressing one or more of these wicked problems.

Darian and her team developed an approach they called SeaChange. It was a comprehensive sustainability strategy that focused on sustainability, safe and legal labor, and responsible sourcing. To implement this strategy, they began to develop a portfolio of partnerships that could help them tackle the wicked problems they faced. Figure 2-1 is a map of Thai Union's partnership portfolio for addressing the wicked problems that the SeaChange strategy was meant to address.

Figure 2-1: Thai Union's Partnership Portfolio

Fair Labor	• Humanity United • International Transport Workers Federation • Verite • Migrant Workers Rights Network • Issara Institute • International Labor Organization • Labor Rights Promotion Network
Seafood Sustainability	• Global Ghost Gear Initiative • WWF • IUCN • Marine Stewardship Council • International Seafood Sustainability Foundation • Greenpeace
Legal and Regulatory	• Global Aquaculture Alliance • USAID • NFI/Crab Council

According to Darian, Thai Union's early collaboration with the Migrant Workers Rights Network (MWRN), a local Thai NGO focused on labor rights, had a particularly positive impact. MWRN brought both a deep knowledge of worker issues and the support of the workforce—two resources that Thai Union needed if it was going to tackle its labor problems. However, the relationship was difficult going at the start. Years of conflict with Thai Union and other major fishing companies had left the MWRN representatives deeply distrustful. Darian described an early meeting over lunch with an MWRN activist this way: "He was so angry, it was half-way through the meal before he began to eat."

To build a new foundation of trust, Thai Union opened up its facilities to inspectors from MWRN. In turn, the MWRN leaders gave specific guidance to Thai Union on improving conditions and establishing systems to ensure that workers' voices were heard. As the two partners built up trust, they expanded their collaboration into new, untested areas, such as worker recruitment. Migrant workers in the seafood industry are often recruited by unscrupulous brokers who charge high fees that the workers are indebted to repay. MWRN helped Thai Union revamp its recruitment policies to help put a stop to these practices.

The partnership has continued to grow and evolve. "MWRN has been there, both holding our hand and being a critical friend the whole time," notes Darian.

Other partnerships were developed over time. Eventually, Thai Union was even able to build a collaboration with one of its harshest and most outspoken critics, the environmental activist organization Greenpeace.

Darian describes how an accidental encounter helped lay the foundation for a new relationship. "Our executive chairman ran into Greenpeace at a tuna industry conference, brought them to the table, and called me. He said, 'Greenpeace is here. Come now. We need to talk.'" Starting with that serendipitous meeting, a series of conversations was launched that took nearly a year. They resulted in an unprecedented agreement between Greenpeace and Thai Union, signed in 2017, focused on improving Thai Union's labor and environmental practices. The two organizations now meet regularly to review progress towards fulfillment of the agreement.

Today (2020), the business benefits of SeaChange and its portfolio of partnerships are clear. While Thai Union still faces the same core set of wicked problems, it has made real progress in addressing them. The network of partners the company has built provide unique skills, expertise, and capabilities in helping solve those wicked problems. The media attacks on Thai Union have subsided. Instead, the company has received numerous accolades for its new approach, including being named the number one food products company in sustainability by the Dow Jones Sustainability Index and the FTSE4Good Index, two of the most respected global organizations tracking the business practices of corporations. Darian McBain herself was recently named Asia's top Sustainability Superwoman by CSRWorks International, a respected sustainability consulting firm.

The situation Darian faced when she arrived at Thai Union may have been extreme, but it is a great example of how a company can clearly define a set of wicked problems and then work in collaboration across sectors to try to address those problems. Other successful companies have used a similar approach to transform seemingly insurmountable challenges into smaller, more manageable issues that can be tackled with the help of like-minded partners.

In the words of PepsiCo's Margaret Henry, "We always have to find ways to make problems into bite-sized chunks where we can see progress along the way." The process of problem analysis and partner identification we've sketched in this chapter suggests how this can work.

Five Reasons *Not* to Partner

Life is short, and partnerships are time-consuming. They also involve significant transaction costs for all parties involved. Therefore, it's important to recognize when an approach other than partnership may be a better path to a solution. Here are five very valid—and very common—reasons *not* to forge a partnership.

"We can solve the problem on our own." If your company understands the problem at hand and has a solution (or has access to it), then do the world a favor and just get on with it. There is no need to forge a partnership in this case.

"The main thing we need is good PR." By its nature, positive public relations is a very ephemeral thing. Therefore, it isn't a strong primary motivation for building a partnership. While good PR might be one outcome of a successful, well-executed partnership, it is generally difficult for a company to maintain interest and commitment to a project over months or years, as required by most partnerships, solely on the basis of PR considerations.

"We have everything we need to implement our idea except for the money." If you are just looking for other people's money

to fund your company's idea, that is what is referred to in the nonprofit world as *fundraising*. There is nothing wrong with fundraising, but it is different from a partnership, in which two or more organizations work together on planning and executing a project based on shared interests and goals.

"We want someone else to shoulder all the risk." Partners share risks and responsibilities jointly. If you are looking to shift the risk of failure for a new project or initiative to an outside party, a partnership is not appropriate.

"A partnership would be a great way to implement our idea, but getting buy-in from our own people is going to be difficult or impossible." Getting and maintaining internal buy-in for a partnership is a challenge in many companies, which is why we've dedicated a whole chapter to the topic later in this book. However, if you are unable to generate internal buy-in within your firm, do yourself and your potential partners a favor—don't try to partner. Under the circumstances, an attempt to forge a partnership is only likely to produce frustration for everyone involved.

Now that you've gotten a feeling for considering whether and how to launch a cross-sector partnership, we're ready to delve into the partnership-building process. In the chapters that follow, we'll dive deep into the mechanics of building and managing impactful cross-sector partnerships to address the complicated and wicked problems your company is facing.

3

Models for Cross-Sector Partnerships

- o Four common models for cross-sector partnerships
- o The advantages and disadvantages offered by each model
- o How to choose the most appropriate model for solving the problem you face

Dateline: The Hague. If ever there was a truly wicked business problem, it is the global issue of consumer and industrial waste. In the pursuit of convenience and low cost, we have built an economy that places a premium on disposable products and packaging. For the better part of a century, planned obsolescence—that is, the designing of products with a limited lifespan that would need to be disposed of within a set period of time—was a cornerstone of corporate strategy across numerous industries, including electronics, apparel, consumer products, automobiles, and pharmaceuticals.

For companies, post-consumer waste has been someone else's problem for decades. Not anymore. Food and beverage companies are now being hammered by consumers for using too much plastic that ends up clogging our waterways and filling our landfills. Consumer goods companies are being pressured by governments and activists to reduce their use of polystyrene. Fast-fashion companies are under tremendous pressure from NGOs to change their business models to reduce the discarding of clothing.

One possible answer to our pollution and waste problems is the idea of the *circular economy*. According to the Ellen MacArthur Foundation, the circular economy "aims to redefine growth, focusing on positive society-wide benefits. It entails gradually decoupling economic activity from the consumption of finite resources and designing waste out of the system." In other words, the circular economy is about using less and reusing more—a lot more—all while enabling companies to grow and consumers to enjoy the products that they love and depend upon.

The circular economy sounds great in principle, but how do we make it a reality? It requires more than a simple project or program; it requires a real sea change in political policies, corporate strategy, and consumer behaviors. As PepsiCo's Simon Lowden puts it, "The circular economy is brutally hard because it is so multi-disciplined. It requires consumer action, infrastructure to collect the right way, technology to convert collection into usable material, manufacturers to incorporate the material, and industry to use the material without compromising the quality and safety of the product. It is a multifaceted beast." Because it requires governments, companies, and NGOs to both collaborate and work independently, the transition to the circular economy requires a movement.

Few people are as passionate about the potential of and the challenges to the circular economy as David McGinty. David is global director of the Platform for Accelerating the Circular Economy (PACE), a coalition of companies, governments, NGOs, and foundations whose mission is to drive public-private action and collaboration to accelerate the transition to a global circular economy. Launched by the World Economic Forum in 2018 and headquartered at The Hague, PACE is chaired jointly by Frans van Houten, the CEO of Philips, the Dutch consumer and health technology company, and Naoko Ishi, the CEO of the Global Environmental Facility, a leading funder of environmental and conservation projects around the world. In the words of van Hauten, "No single organization can drive this transition alone. The biggest impact will come from collective action on a global scale. Companies, governments, and NGOs have to come together to truly co-create the future." The goal of PACE is to help drive this massive cross-sector partnership.

David McGinty puts the purpose of PACE in practical terms. "We are trying to get people to believe in a new vision for the world," he says, "and then try to help organizations take the transitional steps needed to move toward that new world." A lawyer by training with an easy southern drawl and thoughtful demeanor, David came to PACE with a wealth of cross-sector partnership experience in the United States, Africa, and around the world. While working with World Vision, a leading humanitarian NGO, David helped pioneer partnerships with companies to support the organization's programs. As the head of social innovations at Palladium, an international development consultancy, David built investment and cross-sector partnerships in areas such as agriculture, health, and the environment.

"I fell in love with the idea of marrying social good with the business purpose of companies," David says. "Now my career has extended from the most granular, transactional partnerships to the broadest coalition-building with the ambition to create social movements."

At PACE, David is seeking to engage a wide range of disparate actors—companies, NGOs, host governments, and philanthropies—to align around the high-level vision of the circular economy and then to act accordingly, both individually and through partnerships.

PACE does this by working in three areas: leadership, learning, and projects. PACE's leadership group, which consists of CEOs, government ministers, and heads of leading NGOs, works to define an agenda around the circular economy that the member companies, governments, and organizations can rally around. On the learning front, PACE experts scan research and publications on the circular economy, distilling insights into actionable knowledge in specific areas of the economy, including plastics, electronics, agriculture, and apparel. On the project side, PACE serves as a launch platform, convener, and coordinator for a number of joint project partnerships.

PACE is an example of a partnership model called *collective impact*. Popularized by consultants and social entrepreneurship experts Mark Kramer and John Kania, collective impact is defined as "the commitment of a group of actors from different sectors to a common agenda for solving a specific social problem, using a structured form of collaboration." PACE is using the collective impact model because the nature of the circular economy challenge requires operating at multiple levels, driving fundamental changes to corporate strategy and government policy.

On the one hand, PACE needs to win support from leaders at the highest levels of business and government; in David's words, "We need to get CEO and minister-level buy-in as a precursor to induce action at scale." On the other hand, PACE also needs to increase consumer awareness of issues such as plastic waste through efforts like the Global Plastics Action Partnership, which is focused on keeping plastic out of the world's oceans. This partnership brings together companies like Coca-Cola, PepsiCo, and Dow along with the World Bank and several European governments around the goal of reducing the volume of plastic entering waste streams in countries such as Indonesia and Ghana by up to 70 percent over the next five years. The collective action model, which is the most complex type of cross-sector partnership, is the model best suited to this sort of multilevel activity.

Collective impact is just one of four models for structuring cross-sector partnerships. The models range from relatively simple, transactional relationships to the kind of multifaceted and multidimensional collaboration that PACE exemplifies.

From Transactional to Transformative: Four Partnership Models

If we think of cross-sector partnerships as a tool, the best analogy would be the Swiss Army knife, which contains a number of tools—pliers, screwdriver, awl, can opener—all of which may be used to fix different things. Like the Swiss Army knife, a partnership comes in a variety of models, which should be selected based on the problem you're trying to solve and the partners you seek to work with. Figure 3-1 shows four models for partnership and defines some of their core attributes.

Figure 3-1: Cross-Sector Partnership Models

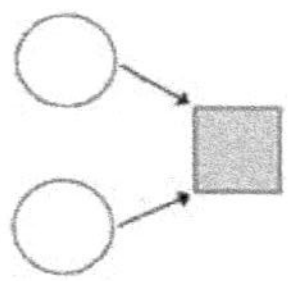

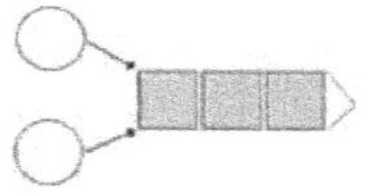

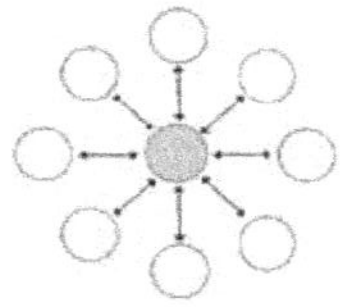

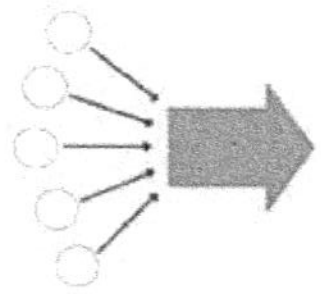

Joint Project

Short-term, one-time collaborative effort or single project

Joint Program

Multiple projects, work streams, or deliverables around a single focus area with a small set of partners

Multi-Stakeholder Initiative

Partners and resources aligned to drive systemic change on a common agenda; often requires a secretariat and a governance structure

Collective Impact

Long-term commitments to a common agenda, with many actors and independent workstreams

Just as choosing the right business model is essential for a startup company to succeed, it's critical to select the right partnership model to address the problem you are seeking to solve. Here is a quick overview of the four partnership models.

The Joint Project

A *joint project* is ideal for tackling relatively straightforward situations involving a problem that, while complicated, is isolated in geography and time. The Texaco case from chapter one is an example. Texaco partnered with the Eurasia Foundation to solve a thorny problem, but the partner relationship itself was a simple one, limited to the narrow confines of the law library and Internet center in Western Kazakhstan.

Joint projects typically involve a small number of partners—often just a single company and a nonprofit or government partner—that agree to work together on a project designed to address a single problem. Because of the small number of partners, the governance and management structures for these partnerships are generally quite straightforward.

Joint projects have some limitations and risks. First, joint projects are fundamentally transactional in nature, involving a simple *quid pro quo* between the partners. This means the partners may not establish deep, collaborative relationships. Second, the small number of partners means that joint projects have concentration risk: If one of the partners drops out or fails to deliver, it is usually fatal to the partnership.

A joint project makes sense when:

- o The problem, though complicated, is limited by time and/or geography

- o A small set of partners—often a single company and one NGO or donor—are ready and able to tackle the problem
- o There is no need or desire for a long-term collaboration; once the problem is solved, the partners can simply move on

The Joint Program

By comparison with a joint project, a *joint program* is broader in scope, typically has a longer time horizon, and may involve multiple partners. The Sri Lanka Easy Seva partnership, which we'll describe in the next chapter, is a good example of a joint program with a wide range of partners—companies, NGOs, and a donor agency—working together over a few years.

A joint program often involves a series of interrelated projects, coordinated and supported by the partners, focused on achieving a discrete, well-defined goal. The program often employs a third-party partnership manager to help coordinate activities, monitor work streams, and convene partners for governance and decision-making purposes. A joint program allows individual organizations to join the partnership to support a particular work stream, then drop off when that work stream is complete. However, the program often relies on a single, highly committed partner to champion the effort from start to finish. If that partner loses interest or is simply unable to continue to drive the partnership, the collaboration can fall apart.

A joint program makes sense when:

- o The problem, though complicated or wicked, is limited by geography and/or time; however, it may require activities over an extended period of time, typically years
- o Multiple partners may join or leave the partnership as needed or desired
- o A committed partner is ready and able to champion the program for as long as needed

The Multi-Stakeholder Initiative

A *multi-stakeholder initiative* brings together a large number of partners around a complicated or wicked problem that can be solved through one or a few clearly defined solutions. For example, the Clean Cooking Alliance is dedicated to helping the three billion people around the world who face health and environmental issues caused by smoky or polluting cookstoves. The alliance focuses on making improved cookstoves that pollute less and are more efficient widely available in the developing world.

The multi-stakeholder initiative is typically composed of a large number of partners across a range of sectors—business, government, NGOs, foundations, and so on. It is typically managed by a centralized team often known as a *secretariat*. The Clean Cooking Alliance, for example, has more than a dozen partners that channel their funding and support through a 30-person secretariat, hosted at the UN Foundation in Washington, D.C., which manages funds and implements programs on behalf of the partners.

Multi-stakeholder initiatives started emerging around the turn of the century in the global health space to tackle issues, such as the HIV/AIDS pandemic and other infectious diseases, where funding can be pooled to drive solutions at scale. The Global Alliance for Vaccines and Immunizations (GAVI), for example, has enabled tens of millions of children in developing countries to be immunized. A multi-stakeholder initiative often requires significant funding for economies of scale to be achieved—typically tens of millions of dollars. Thus, the partners in a multi-stakeholder initiative are often well-heeled funders who may not have the expertise or capability to work on the problem directly. A well-staffed and well-run secretariat, usually run by or organized as an NGO, can provide that capability.

However, when a company's ability to make philanthropic contributions is limited, but it has valuable resources of other kinds to contribute—such as technology, expertise, supply chains, or distribution channels—then working through a secretariat may end up being frustrating.

What's more, agency-principal problems can emerge in which the secretariat acts more in its self-interest than on behalf of the partners who are providing the funding—for example, by focusing on self-perpetuating strategies that will keep the partnership alive regardless of the partners' preferences. Given this risk, when considering a multi-stakeholder initiative, it is critical to have an exit strategy in place from day one.

A multi-stakeholder initiative makes sense when:

- The problem is complicated or wicked and large in scale, involving many countries or geographies
- There is a relatively discrete set of solutions that partners agree upon
- There is a need to coordinate organizations and companies already working on the issue

- o Multiple partners have already stepped up or are ready to commit large amounts of resources, including funding
- o Pooling of funding or activities will enable economies of scale and greater results than if partners acted on their own

The Collective Impact Initiative

As David McGinty's experience with PACE illustrates, collective impact initiatives tend to be quite complex. They involve multiple partners and relationships, some very loose and others very complex, all working toward system-level change, but often independent of one another. Far more than funding, partners bring to a collective impact initiative a range of interests, resources, and capabilities. A collective impact initiative is often used to tackle multifaceted society-level problems, where a wide range of actors work together in a variety of ways. Thus, founding a collective impact initiative is less like starting a problem-solving project and more like launching a movement.

Collective impact initiatives emerged organically in the United States in the late 1980s, with early efforts being focused on wicked problems like smoking cessation, where there was a clear common agenda demanding action to be taken at multiple levels, from grassroots to global. What makes a collective impact partnership unique is the decentralized nature of its structure, in which partners work independently but in coordination with other partners in support of the shared agenda. By setting a common agenda while still catalyzing independent action by a wide range of partners, a collective impact initiative can help to create critical mass, allowing a movement to act with some level of coherence and coordination.

There are five essential elements to a collective impact initiative.

Some level of agreement on a common agenda. Collective impact requires partners to forge a common broad understanding about a problem and develop a shared agenda towards solving it.

Readiness to engage in coordinated, mutually reinforcing activities. In collective impact, partners advance their activities in coordination with other partners with the goal of amplifying their impact.

Willingness to develop a shared measurement system. Partners need to agree upon data collection methods, success indicators, and performance measures, so that activities under the collective impact initiative can be aligned and partners held to account.

Open communication. Despite the decentralized natural of collective impact Initiatives, partners must have open communication across the partners and with stakeholders.

A backbone organization. Collective impact partnerships generally require what's called a *backbone organization*—often an NGO—that serves as a convener and coordinator. In the case of PACE, David and his small team of three are hosted by the World Resources Institute (WRI), a U.S.-based environmental think tank that serves as the backbone organization. The backbone organization is not a secretariat designed to channel funding and implement activities, as found in a multi-stakeholder initiative. Rather, the role of the backbone is to bring the key stakeholders together, help set a common agenda, and serve as a coordinator across multiple, often independent work streams.

The leader of a backbone organization needs to combine the skills of a diplomat, a PR professional and a project manager.

A collective impact initiative makes sense when:

- o The problem is truly wicked and requires action at multiple levels—local, national, and international
- o There is no single solution or solution set; instead, solving the problem requires multiple types of activities across government, business, and civil society, and there are a large number of organizations—NGOs, companies, government agencies—already actively working on the problem, although their work is not coordinated
- o It is not feasible or desirable to centralize the work of partners, but there is a need for some coordination and convening to ensure broad alignment even as partners act independently

As with any movement that involves multiple actors working independently, collective impact initiatives can be challenging to manage and govern. Their loose structure and independent work streams create risks of duplication or even working at cross-purposes.

Note that individual companies rarely, if ever, instigate the creation of a collective impact initiative. Instead, collective impact initiatives frequently emerge from the nonprofit sector and often have a strong grassroots orientation. Thus, for-profit companies, particularly large multinational corporations, are not well positioned to initiate a collective impact effort, but they can be early adopters and leaders once the initiative is underway.

Given the truly global, multifaceted nature of the problem it is trying to solve, PACE needs to help set and shape a global agenda among a wide array of companies, NGOs, foundations, and governments. For this reason, a collective impact model was likely the only viable option.

Choosing the Right Model

These four partnership models—joint project, joint program, multi-stakeholder initiative, and collective impact—should be considered points along a continuum rather than mutually exclusive designs with no overlap. Some partnerships combine characteristics of two or more models. For example, within the PACE collective impact partnership, there are a number of joint projects and programs taking place. Partnerships can also evolve into different models over time.

Getting the partnership model right is critical because building a partnership—even a relatively straightforward joint project—can be a very time-consuming process that requires repeated experiments and modifications in response to changing circumstances. If you start with an ill-considered choice of model, you may end up wasting needless time, money, and other resources.

Remember the classic design dictum first articulated by architect Louis Henry Sullivan, "Form follows function." Once you are clear on the problem you are trying to solve, clarity of purpose then informs the shape of the partnership you should build.

But, in addition, be ready to pivot. As you begin to work on the problem and engage with partners, you may find that your initial partnership model proves to be inadequate. In that case, you need to be ready to move to a different partnership model.

As of this writing, PACE's collective impact partnership is barely a year old, so it is far too early to know whether its ambitious vision of transitioning our single-use, disposable economy to a circular economy will succeed. It will likely be many years—perhaps decades—before we can measure the extent to which PACE will have succeeded in moving the needle. However, PACE's ability to gather and engage the right stakeholders at various levels is a promising first step.

4

The Arc of a Partnership: The LABS Framework

- o The stages in the process of building and managing a cross-sector partnership
- o The Learn, Align, Build, Scale/Sustain (LABS) framework for partnerships

Dateline: Sri Lanka. In late 2006, I found myself in a small town in rural Sri Lanka, standing on a bustling village street corner as three-wheeled *tuk tuks* putted by and children in neat, British-style uniforms walked in pairs and groups to the nearby school. This was my first of what would become many visits to the island country, and I was just beginning to discover Sri Lanka's seductive charm, born of its warm hospitality, rich culture, and lush landscapes. But at the moment I was lost in thought, mulling over the dilemma confronting me.

My firm, then called SSG Advisors, which I had founded only one year before, had just been hired to try to solve a major challenge: how to deliver affordable broadband internet to rural communities where the average income was roughly $50 per month. The technology of the day seemed inadequate. The iPhone would not be introduced for another year, and 3G, considered cutting edge, wasn't widely available even in the United States. Internet access in rural areas in Sri Lanka was limited, expensive, and available only via dial-up for a cost of about $2.50 per hour for a tortoise-like 64 kilobits-per-second connection. It also required a PC and a landline, both rare commodities in rural Sri Lankan homes. Let's not even talk about cable or fiber.

What's more, our project had a total budget of less than $400,000 for salaries, travel, equipment, transportation—everything. But we were expected to have everything up, running, and sustainable in at least 20 communities across the country within a year.

Delivering universal Internet access is a great example of a complicated problem. By 2019, despite the incredible proliferation of smart phones around the world, only 50 percent of the world's population had online connections to the Internet. The vast majority of the unconnected are poor and live in rural areas with low population density, which means there are few customers for every cell tower or telephone pole, thus driving up the cost for people with the least ability to pay. As our economic and political worlds become increasingly digitally intermediated, those unconnected millions are increasingly left behind, creating greater inequality and the potential for social and political instability. As the world's population spirals upward toward ten billion, the digital divide could well become a digital chasm.

Internet access is not just a business challenge—it is also an opportunity. For companies like Facebook and Google, the more eyeballs there are on the Internet, the greater their revenue. That's why they have invested hundreds of millions of dollars in elaborate schemes to connect the unconnected using everything from drones to helium balloons.

In the mid-2000s, the United States Agency for International Development (USAID) partnered with a group of companies to figure out how to bring the Internet to rural communities in Sri Lanka, one of the least-developed countries in Asia. The partners hoped that this project could show how the complicated problem of universal Internet access might be solved more generally. In this chapter, we'll explore how this partnership came together, how it was managed, and what it achieved. Along the way, we'll introduce the Learn, Align, Build, Scale/Sustain (LABS) framework for developing and managing partnerships to deliver social impact and business value.

Solving the complicated problem of rural broadband access in Sri Lanka with very limited budget resources required a creative approach. The approach we ultimately settled on was a cross-sector partnership. We would identify and bring in partners from industry, government, and the nonprofit sector who had the capabilities, resources, and incentives to work with us to solve the problem. Over the course of the next year, we would bring on multinational companies, like QUALCOMM and Microsoft; a local mobile operator called Dialog; a donor agency; a local NGO; and dozens of local entrepreneurs.

Working as partners, we developed and deployed a network of Internet café microfranchises to more than 50 rural communities across Sri Lanka, connecting more than 100,000 rural consumers to broadband at the then-amazing price of 37 cents per megabit—two orders of magnitude better than what was previously available using dial-up. We tested the real-world efficacy of new technologies like 3G and WiMAX. In the process, we demonstrated that rural base-of-the-pyramid consumers had a high appetite and willingness to pay for quality telecommunications services if they could be delivered at the right price.

The process of identifying, building, and managing this complex cross-sector partnership was not an easy one. There were many bumps, false starts, and near-death experiences along the way. The survival of the project was a testament to the dedication of the partners and their commitment to see the journey through to a successful end.

In this chapter, we'll use the lens of the Sri Lanka experience to explore the components of LABS (Figure 4-1). The goal will be to provide a holistic overview of how companies and organizations can build and manage cross-sector partnerships. In the chapters that follow, we'll take a deep dive into the different components of LABS through our analysis of a number of other impressive partnerships.

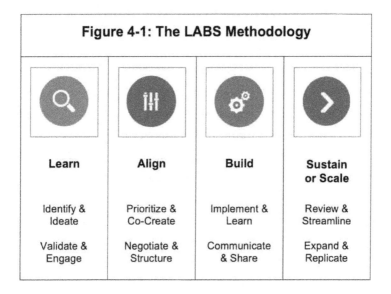

Figure 4-1: The LABS Methodology

Learn	Align	Build	Sustain or Scale
Identify & Ideate	Prioritize & Co-Create	Implement & Learn	Review & Streamline
Validate & Engage	Negotiate & Structure	Communicate & Share	Expand & Replicate

Learn (1): Identify & Ideate

When SSG Advisors won the Sri Lanka project from USAID, we were a bit like the barking dog that finally catches the car it has been chasing: We were excited to have captured our prey, but we weren't quite sure what to do next. We were not telecommunications experts, and we had very little knowledge of Sri Lanka. However, we did have a pretty good understanding of the problem USAID was trying to solve—making sustainable Internet access more broadly available in rural areas. As I recounted in chapter one, I had helped to build public-access Internet centers across Central Asia. That experience taught me that, without an underlying business model to support the costs of connectivity and the maintenance of equipment and systems, such Internet centers had great difficulty sustaining themselves when the donor funding ran out. Many could not afford the then-high cost of Internet connectivity.

So we knew that donor or philanthropic money might be necessary but insufficient to solve the problem. But we also saw the potential of the useful assets USAID was bringing to the table: significant funding, project management capabilities, and the convening authority of the U.S. government. We understood the problem we needed to solve, we knew we couldn't solve it alone, and we had defined the assets available to us. We were ready to start the search for partners.

At this point, we began to follow the LABS methodology, starting with the first step—Learn—and its two subparts: Identify & Ideate and Validate & Engage.

We dedicated our first trip to Sri Lanka to getting the lay of the land. I was joined by two other team members. Tony Nash, now founder and CEO of Complete Intelligence, was between jobs at the time this project was launched. Tony and I had gone to grad school together and become lifelong friends. He is one of the smartest people I have ever met and has a strong background in telecommunications in Asia, an essential expertise for our purposes. Tony signed on as team leader.

We were joined by Shoban Rainford, now business development director at SNV, a Dutch NGO dedicated to pursuing the United Nations' Sustainable Development Goals (SDGs). Having grown up between Sri Lanka and the United Kingdom, Shoban was a thoughtful, committed, and insightful resource who helped Tony and me to navigate the nuances of the Sri Lankan business and civil society communities. Shoban served as our on-the-ground project manager and eventually led the project.

As our telecommunications industry guru, Tony first identified a number of industry trends that were shaping the marketplace into which we hoped to move.

Sri Lanka's dominant mobile operator at the time, Dialog Telekom, had been an early mover into 2G and had invested aggressively to expand its network nationwide. Now, however, there were a number of new wireless connectivity technologies coming to market—notably 3G and WiMAX—that could connect remote communities far less expensively than traditional copper wire networks. Sri Lanka had just issued its first licenses for 3G and WiMax the year before.

In addition, Intel's then-new Atom processor was driving down the entry-level price of PCs and laptops to below $200, representing a huge decline in price of a key piece of equipment.

Finally, competition in the mobile network business in South Asia was rapidly increasing, with several Indian operators, notably AirTel, signaling that they planned to enter the Sri Lanka market.

Tony's macro-level market analysis provided us with extremely useful background as we began to explore the possibilities for Sri Lanka. When carrying out the LABS process, we use this type of rapid macroanalysis to help us ground ourselves in the realities of the marketplace.

To get an even deeper understanding of the realities that our potential customers in rural Sri Lanka were facing, we traveled to several villages and interviewed practically anyone who would talk to us—shopkeepers, school teachers, parents, local officials, and more—using some simple, open-ended interview techniques. We quickly learned a number of important facts about the current market.

First, the high cost of an Internet connection and the required financial commitment was virtually impossible for most individual consumers in Sri Lanka. This was a country where incomes were low, typically in the range of $50 to 100 per month.

However, telecommunication was a high priority for many families, especially those who had loved ones working overseas, for example in the countries of the Persian Gulf. Remittances from those overseas workers were a crucial part of the budget for many Sri Lankan households. In response to this demand, 2G mobile telephones were proliferating rapidly as mobile networks built base stations and established local dealers who could provide quick and affordable top-ups for SIM-card memory chips. This market growth showed that local villagers were willing and able to pay for telecommunications provided the quality was high and the price was moderate.

Finally, we learned that interest in education was universally high across every community and demographic: women, men, children, municipal officials, and others.

Armed with these insights, Tony, Shoban, and I began to brainstorm on how we could approach the project and potentially engage partners. You might picture us working on a whiteboard in an innovation lab, but, in reality, we did most of our early planning by scribbling on beer-soaked napkins during our evenings at a favorite oceanside bar.

Our thinking was driven by a handful of critical assumptions.

Given the willingness of Sri Lankan consumers to pay for Internet for communications and educational purposes, as well as the increasing competition in the mobile network space, we suspected that one or more mobile network operators (MNOs) might be interested in exploring creative new ways to offer telecommunications services to consumers.

We also believed that the emergence of ultra-low-cost PCs and new wireless connectivity technologies might allow us to overcome the formidable cost barriers by leapfrogging over traditional dial-up business models. The presence of mobile SIM-card top-up dealers in the villages meant there were proven local entrepreneurs who were already offering telecommunications services to their customers. These factors suggested that some form of shared Internet access approach, such as Internet cafés or telecenters, might offer a workable solution.

We began to piece together a concept for a network of microfranchised Internet cafés, connected to the Internet using wireless broadband. To make this happen, three components would need to be developed. Let's sketch out what each of these components were and their implication for what we needed from partners.

Internet cafés. This shared-access model would enable us to amortize the costs of PCs and Internet connections over many customers, allowing us to keep prices low. To create the cafés, we would need local entrepreneurs in the communities who were familiar with technology.

A microfranchising system. The cafés would be fee-for-service businesses using a single predefined business model, technology, and pricing strategy. To create and implement this system, we would need a partner who could deliver a standard product or service across Sri Lanka.

Wireless broadband (3G or WiMAX). By leapfrogging traditional copper wire telephone infrastructure, we could reach more villages more quickly and cheaply. This would require a wireless mobile operator or an Internet service provider (ISP) as a core operator—one with the necessary licenses, network infrastructure, and technical support capabilities.

This brainstorming process gave us a working hypothesis for a potential solution that could deliver rural Internet access to the people of Sri Lanka at sufficient scale to be sustainable. Developing such a working hypothesis early in the LABS process is extremely useful, because it gives you a tentative problem-solving model that can be tested, validated or disproven, and either deployed more broadly or replaced with an improved model.

Learn (2): Validate & Engage

Next, Tony and Shoban pulled together a series of about thirty meetings over the course of a week, through which we tested our working hypothesis. We met with mobile network companies, representatives of western tech companies, philanthropic donors, government officials, and NGO leaders to ascertain whether our tentative model might create opportunities to collaborate. In these interviews, we asked a few very basic open-ended questions.

- o What are your organization's goals for the next five years?
- o What challenges keep you and the executives of your organization up at night?
- o In what ways could delivering expanded Internet access to rural Sri Lankans help your organization achieve your goals and address your challenges?

The answers to these questions helped us better understand the goals and risks dominating the thinking of our potential partners—elements that might provide strong incentives for them to work collaborate with us.

We also provided a brief thumbnail sketch of our proposed solution—the microfranchised Internet café model. From those initial conversations, we identified about a dozen potential partners, all of whom were motivated to help solve the Internet access problem in rural Sri Lanka, brought assets we needed to the effort, and saw value in what we had to offer.

Align (1): Prioritize & Co-Create

Coming out of that initial round of meetings, we were excited. There seemed to be genuine interest in the potential of microfranchised Internet cafés as a tool for delivering broadband to rural Sri Lanka. However, while we saw great potential in the group of potential partners we'd identified, we couldn't yet gauge their willingness to commit to a partnership.

Therefore, we decided to leverage one of our assets: the convening power of the U.S. government, a beneficial effect of being funded by USAID, America's largest foreign aid agency. Robert Blake, the U.S. ambassador to Sri Lanka, graciously offered to host a closed-door roundtable with our potential partners. An invitation to such a meeting with the lead representative of the government of the largest economy on Earth is no small thing, and we knew our potential partners would take it seriously.

The roundtable was a great success. Several companies—most notably Dialog Telekom and QUALCOMM—affirmed their interest in becoming full-fledged partners in our project. Several other organizations also expressed strong interest.

Now it was up to us to put definition around the partnership so that we could move forward. We had to design the partnership; define the roles, responsibilities, and contributions of the participants; and create a joint decision-making structure. Over the course of the next several weeks, Tony and Shoban engaged in an intense period of shuttle diplomacy among the partners as they worked to co-create the structure of what became a joint program aligned around the goal of piloting a new business model for promoting rural Internet access in Sri Lanka.

Align (2): Negotiate & Structure

As each element of the partnership was defined, we codified our understanding through memoranda of understanding (MoUs). In quick order, we signed agreements with Dialog Telekom and QUALCOMM, two core partners that each contributed resources and funding critical to our success. InfoShare, a Sri Lankan NGO focused on human rights and information and communications technology (ICT), was our third partner, providing office space and a nationwide network of contacts in the technology arena. Somewhat later, we brought on additional partners Lanka Orix (a PC equipment leasing company) and Microsoft (which would provide software and training for participants in our budding network of telecenters).

As the partnerships fell into place, Tony and Shoban also had to move quickly to flesh out an action plan that would convert our agreements into results on the ground. They established a simple but rigorous project management structure, scheduled regular check-in calls with the partners to hold one another accountable, and began converting our tentative business model into a concrete business plan. The plan called for a microfranchise system that would use then-cutting-edge 3G technology, provided by Qualcomm and operated by Dialog, to connect a network of Internet cafés to one-megabit-per-second broadband—lightning speed by the standards of the day.

Build (1): Implement & Learn

With MoUs signed and an action plan in place, it was time to begin making things happen. The Build phase is when a partnership begins executing on its plans. It's divided into two subparts: Implement & Learn, and Communicate & Share.

By early spring, 2007, it was time to begin to implement our business plan. Tony and Shoban created a small team to travel to targeted towns and villages to identify promising potential entrepreneurs who could own and operate the Internet cafés using a standard business and operating model. Once an entrepreneur was selected, we helped them apply for an equipment lease on favorable terms from Lanka Orix. Meanwhile, Dialog needed to move quickly to identify tower locations and install 3G antenna. At the same time, Qualcomm needed to work with a vendor (Chinese equipment maker Huawei) to build the latest 3G base stations on Dialog's network.

We now faced some unexpected developments. A promising partnership with Hewlett Packard to provide printers never materialized because the company pivoted its business model in a different direction. Then Tony was offered a very attractive job with the Economist Intelligence Unit, the type of once-in-a-lifetime career opportunity that Tony couldn't refuse. Luckily for us, Tony would continue to help out when he could on nights and weekends, but he was unable to commit large chunks of time. To lead the team, we brought in Darrell Owen, a highly experienced former USAID telecommunications expert, to work in tandem with Shoban.

These unexpected changes forced us to adapt on the fly to changing circumstances. To help us navigate the rapidly changing context, we developed a simple measuring and learning framework to help us ensure alignment among partners, coordinate activities, and track results. (More on developing this kind of framework in chapter nine.)

In May, 2007, less than a year after launching our project, we celebrated the gala opening of the first Easy Seva Internet center in Matale, Sri Lanka. The center quickly became a popular local destination. Over the course of the summer, Shoban, Darrell, and their team opened 21 more centers across rural Sri Lanka. Qualcomm and USAID were so pleased that they increased our funding by $250,000. Meanwhile, Dialog Telekom expanded its technical support and 3G network, paving the way for us to open dozens more centers.

Build (2): Communicate & Share

In any partnership, it's critical for the partners to communicate effectively with each other and with outside stakeholders. It's also important for partners to be consulted and engaged in decision-making. In our Sri Lanka project, we used a few simple approaches to meet these challenges.

First, we had a standing weekly project management call to review tasks, activities, issues, and risks to successful implementation. While all partners were welcome to participate, in practice, Dialog Telekom—one of our core partners—was the only one to participate on a regular basis. Others took part from time to time as necessary.

We also had a monthly all-partners conference call that focused on higher-level decision-making regarding the location of new Easy Seva Internet cafés, key performance indicators, and other matters of general importance. This kept all the partners actively engaged in the work and enabled our team to leverage the expertise and networks of our partners.

We also worked to build ongoing communications with our growing network of Easy Seva center owner/operators. To build trust, we deployed a small team of specialists to visit each Easy Seva center and to meet with the owner/operator to troubleshoot technology issues (of which there were many) and provide mentoring on how to improve services for customers. These face-to-face visits built trust and provided us with a valuable feedback loop, enabling us to have a strong sense of what was working and what was not.

Sustain or Scale

By the summer of 2008, we had opened 55 Easy Seva centers—more than double our original forecast. The centers were also profitable and therefore sustainable. Feeling we had the wind at our backs, we developed an ambitious business plan to scale Easy Seva throughout Sri Lanka and ultimately across Asia.

However, we faced a number of challenges. First, we were having great difficulty collecting franchising fees to support the central operation. This was in the days before mobile money, so we were relying on cash collections, which were time-consuming, costly to collect, and less than reliable. Thus, although the centers themselves were profitable, the Easy Seva franchise system was running in the red and burning through our very precious funds very quickly.

In addition, a long-simmering civil war in Sri Lanka was rapidly heating up in 2008. The fighting made it difficult for Easy Seva entrepreneurs in the northern and eastern portions of the country. The growing conflict also started to make our partners nervous about continuing the project in the face of political instability.

After several failed efforts to raise more capital to finance the expansion of Easy Seva, we reviewed the situation with our partners and concluded that expansion simply was not realistic under these circumstances. We also decided that the only way Easy Seva could survive was to transition the operation to the one partner that had the expertise, incentive, and capabilities to ensure long-term support of the Easy Seva Centers: Dialog Telekom.

This was a painful conclusion for us to reach. Our team and our partners had poured their hearts and souls into Easy Seva.

Fortunately, Dialog, seeing the Easy Seva Centers as a useful tool for expanding their brand in rural areas, graciously agreed to take over responsibility for managing the operation.

In late 2008, we signed the paperwork signing over Easy Seva to Dialog, which has continued to support the existing network of entrepreneurs. According to an independent study, more than 80 percent of the Easy Seva centers were profitable more than six months after the dissolution of the partnership, meaning we had created sustainable businesses capable of delivering affordable Internet access to more than 100,000 people in rural Sri Lanka.

I was disappointed that we weren't able to scale Easy Seva to its fullest potential. But it's clear that the effort was a major success. We showed that it was possible to provide a sustainable solution to the complicated, multifaceted problem of providing rural Internet access in low-income countries.

The project was also successful for each of our key partners. For Dialog Telekom, it demonstrated the potential of the rural customer base if provided with compelling service at an affordable price point. For QUALCOMM, the partnership represented the first fixed deployment of 3G technology, proving the capability of the technology to deliver broadband in a challenging real-world setting. For Microsoft, the partnership demonstrated the potential of public Internet centers to be a focal point for the skills-building needed to get new users up to speed on Microsoft software. For USAID, Easy Seva became a lighthouse project, illustrating the power of partnerships and the value of a market-based solution to development challenges.

Most important, the residents of the towns and villages where Easy Seva opened centers enjoyed access to quality Internet at a price many could afford. Students began using the centers to study for their exams. Overseas workers used the centers to submit paperwork to embassies and consulates in the capital city of Colombo. An online match-making service emerged. Even local businesses began to use the centers to communicate with customers and vendors elsewhere in the country. Easy Seva demonstrated the potential of the rural base-of-the-pyramid market for Internet services.

The Winding Partnership Road

The Easy Seva partnership highlights both the promise and the challenges of cross-sector collaboration. The eventful journey by which we transformed a bare-bones concept into a partnership that delivered affordable Internet access to rural communities for the first time showed how thoughtfully designed partnerships can deliver results for companies, government agencies, and communities alike.

In the chapters that follow, we'll take a deeper dive into each component of LABS through the experiences of business professionals like you. You'll see how companies have found ways to tackle complicated and even wicked problems through cross-sector partnerships, building business value in the process. You'll also be introduced to tools and approaches that can make your journey easier and your partnerships more effective and results-focused.

5

From Problem to Partnership

- o   Defining the problem to be solved by your cross-sector partnership
- o   Identifying potential partners
- o   Creating profiles of potential partners
- o   Engaging potential partners
- o   Developing and iterating a partnership hypothesis

Dateline: Ghana and Kenya. Most people know that heart disease is the number one killer in the United States and many other developed countries. But did you know that it is quickly emerging as a leading cause of premature death in sub-Saharan Africa? In Kenya, for example, heart disease is responsible for fully a quarter of hospital admissions and is emerging as a leading cause of premature death among adults. The prevalence of heart disease and other noncommunicable diseases (NCDs) is only expected to grow in coming years, presenting a huge public health challenge in countries where the health care infrastructure is struggling to keep up with demand.

This is a problem that Chemu Lang'at of Medtronic Labs Global Health knows well. A biomedical engineer by training, Chemu began her career at NASA, where she helped design medical monitoring devices and exercise equipment for use by astronauts on the international space station. She then moved to Medtronic, where she planned to focus on designing new medical devices.

However, her plans changed when the Medtronic launched an innovation competition focused on ways the company could generate business value while improving health outcomes for marginalized populations, like those in developing countries. Much to her delight, Chemu's team was selected as one of the winners of the innovation competition, and the team was given the opportunity to bring their ideas to life.

But as Chemu and the Medtronic Labs team dug deeper into the problem of cardiovascular health in Africa, they realized

77

that the problem they were trying to solve was much more complicated than they'd realized.

Getting Clear on the Problem to be Solved: The Five Whys Technique

Every cross-sector partnership has a unique origin story. But all partnership origin stories begin with a problem to be defined, and then solved.

Problem definition may seem simple, but that superficial impression can be very misleading. It's not uncommon for long-term partners to find themselves operating at cross-purposes because they have been unwittingly focused on different problems.

Some years ago, I was asked to evaluate a partnership focused on improving seed markets in West Africa. The partners included several seed companies, a seed association, a donor agency, and a large foundation. I soon discovered that there was significant tension among the partners—in fact, in one meeting during the evaluation, I had to mediate a shouting match between two key leaders.

When I asked the partners to describe the underlying problem they were seeking to solve, the cause of the tension became clear. The seed companies and the donor agency saw the problem as largely a regulatory issue; they were eager to push for loosening restrictions on genetically modified seeds. Meanwhile, the foundation saw the primary problem as getting improved hybrid, non-modified seeds into the hands of farmers, and wanted to avoid getting involved in regulatory issues, especially the controversy around genetically modified organisms (GMOs). The lack of a clear, shared problem definition spelled long-term trouble for the partnership, as we'll explain in chapter ten.

When the Medtronic Labs team got the opportunity to work on the problem of cardiovascular health in Africa, they had hoped their background and expertise with medical technology would be of use in addressing some of the challenges they might unearth. However, through their visits to Ghana (and later Kenya), the team discovered new facets to the problem. The deeper the Medtronic Labs team dug, they more they realized that the problem they were trying to solve was not primarily about access to technology or devices. It was about a problem at the systems level.

The Medtronic team met with a wide range of medical and health systems officials in Ghana, including clinicians, community health workers, and government health officials, to better understand the nature of heart disease in the country. "We asked all these questions about heart failure," Chemu recalls:

> But we kept getting bombarded with problems associated with hypertension [that is, high blood pressure]. There were issues with primary care, with referrals, with admissions, with patient care, and with adherence to medical care plans. There were a lot of concerns around patients being on medication for the rest of their lives. At the end of that trip, over dinner at a restaurant, our team leader asked, "Are we looking at the wrong problem? Maybe we should be looking at hypertension." We realized that if we tackled the issue of hypertension, we might be able to prevent the problem of heart failure in the first place.

The Medtronic Labs team concluded that, in developing countries like Kenya and Ghana, complications from heart disease and other NCDs result from a lack of awareness, late diagnosis of hypertension, and a failure to adhere to care plans. If Medtronic was going to move the needle on the issue of heart disease in Africa, it couldn't simply design lower-cost devices to service the African market. It needed to take a very different approach to address the systemic causes driving the problem of heart disease. When framed through a systems-thinking lens, it became clear that the problem Medtronic was setting out to solve—reducing mortality rates from heart disease and related NCDs in Africa—would require a new model of care for heart disease and hypertension.

In the Medtronic Labs case, the need to rethink assumptions about the nature of the problem became apparent when the team members were confronted with unexpected questions during their initial fact-finding mission. In other cases, the challenge of problem definition arises when team members realize that their preliminary understanding is superficial or incomplete.

An example of this problem is the challenge we discussed in the introduction to this book. As you'll recall, we described how PepsiCo's Sustainable Agriculture team is faced with the problem of increasing the supply and quality of potatoes and other crops in India, while also introducing sustainable farming approaches to secure supply for the long term. It's a complicated problem involving everything from inputs such as seeds, fertilizer, and irrigation to access to finance, growing techniques, local demographic shifts, and global climate change.

In order to crystalize their understanding of the nature of the problem they faced and determine whether a cross-sector partnership could contribute to a solution, the Pepscio Sustainable Agriculture team needed to analyze the problem in terms of root causes and effects. To launch this kind of analysis, the *Five Whys technique* can helpful. It involves asking a series of *why* questions, drilling down below surface phenomena until the underlying causes of the problem are uncovered.

Used with patience, techniques like the Five Whys enabled the PepsiCo Sustainable Agriculture team to get at one of the main root causes of problem the company faced with its India supply chain—particularly with women farmers, who make up a substantial portion of the agricultural work force. The sequence of Five Whys began with the problem to be diagnosed—the fact that PepsiCo's agricultural supply chain in India was struggling to provide the materials needed by the company.

- o *First Why?* Farm yields and crop quality are too low to meet PepsiCo's growing needs.
- o *Second Why?* Farmers are not adopting modern practices or making investments in improvements.
- o *Third Why?* Decisions about farming practices and investment arc largely made by male family members whose thinking about business strategy tends to be driven by traditional practices and short-term focus.
- o *Fourth Why?* Women farmers lack access to information, modern technology, and credit that would enable them to participate more fully in the management of their family's farms.
- o *Fifth Why?* This *why* finally yields a root cause: The exclusion of Indian women from agricultural decision-making, access to credit, and technology is negatively impacting productivity and yields.

The Five Whys technique can help you to get clear on the problem to be solved. Once you dig in deep and get clear on the underlying nature of the problem, you are in a better position to develop an idea about how it might be solved—and also to identify potential partners who might share your interest in solving it.

The Problem in Context: Could We Tackle This Problem on Our Own?

Let's stick with the PepsiCo case for a moment. With the problem defined, the Sustainable Agriculture team then needed to decide whether this was something they could handle themselves. As a leading food and beverage company, PepsiCo has a large team of very capable agronomists working around the world to support farmers in their supply chain. "That's the power of the private sector," notes Margaret Henry. "We have to get stuff done." In addition, the company possesses decades of experience with sourcing in global markets, including in India, and thus brought a rich and nuanced understanding of the country context.

What PepsiCo lacked, however, was an idea of how best to integrate women into their agricultural supply chain in India. As it is in many countries, farming in India is a highly male-dominated activity, and changing the social expectations that underlie traditional attitudes about gender roles in this area would likely be a multifaceted, complicated problem. It didn't take long for the Sustainable Agriculture team to realize that PepsiCo lacked the necessary expertise and resources to solve the problem on its own.

Faced with a different problem, Medtronic reached a similar conclusion. Once they identified treatment of hypertension as the systems-level problem underlying the surface issue of deaths from heart disease, it was clear that this was not an issue that the device-oriented experts at Medtronic could tackle on their own. If Medtronic hoped to generate systemic change in the way hypertension is treated in Africa, the company would need to collaborate with a range of stakeholders up and down the health care value chain, from small village clinics and pharmacies to ministries of health in Nairobi and Accra.

The Problem in Context: Is This a Problem Shared by Others?

Partnerships are fueled on mutual self-interest. That means each partner needs to have a strong self-interest in developing a shared solution to the problem. No one will partner with you to solve *your* problem; partners work together in order to solve their *shared* problem. Thus, a cross-sector partnership only makes sense if the problem to be solved is of interest to a number of parties in industry, government, or civil society.

To understand whether a problem may be shared by others, it is important to place the problem in a context broader than that of your company. In some cases, doing this may be easy. You may be deeply familiar with the problem and the key stakeholders interested in solving it. In other cases, however, it may require some research. As you work to place your problem in context, here a few key questions to consider.

- *What are the economic and social factors influencing the problem?* These may include GDP growth (or lack thereof), unemployment, exports, imports, health outcomes, educational attainment, political conflicts, gender roles, environmental challenges, and so on.
- *What are the key industry trends impacting the problem?* Are those trends likely to continue? Is the impact of these trends on the problem likely to increase or decrease?
- *What are media outlets and influencers saying about this problem?* Are NGO leaders, political figures, and activist groups engaged with the problem? Is this a hot-button issue for other companies or for policymakers? As Ed Martin, the cofounder of the marketing and partnerships firm 5th Element, likes to ask, "Who else wins if I solve this problem?"

When PepsiCo's Margaret Henry and Rob Meyers examined the agricultural yield problem, including its root connection with the lack of influence afforded to women decision-makers in Indian farm families, a number of contextual realities jumped out at them. Based on their understanding of social and political dynamics in the country, they knew that donor agencies, the government of India, and a range of NGOs would likely have a strong interest in empowering women in agriculture. Thus, understanding the problem in context helped PepsiCo understand some of the types of outside organizations that might have a shared interest in helping them solve the problem.

In the case of Medtronic Labs, Chemu Lang'at and her team quickly realized that many components of the health care system in sub-Saharan Africa would share their interest in addressing the problem of heart disease and its root relationship with hypertension at a variety of levels, from national health services and ministries of health down to community clinics, local health care providers, and other stakeholders concerned with community well-being. This meant that Medtronic Labs would have at least a fighting chance to achieving its goal of driving systemic change to reduce the incidence of heart disease throughout the region.

Identifying Potential Partners

With the problem now framed in its context, you can begin to identify specific organizations that may be interested in partnering with you.

Medtronic Labs had a range of initial ideas for potential partners. "We initially started with the ministry of health," Chemu recalls. "Then, as we did the landscape analysis, we visited every single level [of the health care system], and along the way we started building our network. We engaged with nurses and community health workers. We visited patient's homes, and we spent time in the [hospital] wards to understand their experience."

In other cases, you may not even know where to begin to find potential partners. But identifying potential partners is not rocket science. It often requires little more than a laptop, an Internet connection, and an investment of time to conduct preliminary research into who else cares about the problem. Seek out a handful of experts who can describe the types of organizations that are impacted by the problem and may already be working on solving it. Go broad rather than deep. Look at organizations of all kinds: for-profit companies, NGOs, foundations, government agencies, academic and research institutions, civic groups, religious communities, activist organizations, and so on. Your goal is to create a simple but comprehensive map of organizations working on or impacted by the problem.

Figure 5-1 lists typical types of partners along with the pros and cons commonly associated with each.

Figure 5-1: Types of Partner Organizations

Type	Pros	Cons
Bilateral donor agencies	• Project funding • Convening power • Expertise	• May be slow-moving, bureaucratic
Multilateral organizations	• Project funding • Convening power • Expertise • Geographic reach	• Rigid operating structure • Complex application process
Host government agencies	• Policy and regulatory expertise • Convening power • Local knowledge and buy-in	• May be slow-moving, bureaucratic • Limited funding • Goals between ministries may be misaligned

Type	Pros	Cons
Nongovernmental organizations (NGOs)	• Project implementation • Accountability and reputation • Reach into new areas	• Lack of funding support • Mission-focused • May be reluctant to engage
Private foundations	• Project funding • Technical expertise • Innovative thinking	• Mission may be misaligned • Opaque decision process
Development finance institutions (DFIs)	• Financing for supply chains • Credibility • Technical expertise and research • Help with policy reform	• May be slow-moving, bureaucratic • Expect return on investment • Limited partnership experience
Impact investors	• Project funding • Strong existing networks • Innovative thinking	• Narrow investment criteria • Startup overkill • May be faddish

Type	Pros	Cons
Commercial banks	• Project funding	• Expect commercial rate of return • Low scalability • Low historic investment
Universities and research institutions	• Thought leadership • Influence • Advisory support	• Funding dependent on donors • Limited scale • May be suspicious of partner motives
Multinational corporations	• Project funding • Supplier or distribution networks • Innovative products and services • Marketing reach	• Goals may be misaligned • May be perceived as exploitative
Vendors and suppliers	• Technical expertise • Networks	• May not be transparent

Let's dig a bit deeper into the characteristics of some of the most common types of partners.

Bilateral donor agencies. These are government agencies in developed countries that provide aid to developing countries. Aid can come in the form of direct funding to the recipient government (government-to-government, or G2G) or via NGOs and contracting firms (often called *technical assistance*). USAID is the largest U.S. government agency involved in foreign assistance. It has an annual budget of nearly $20 billion and operates in close to 80 countries around the world. Other prominent bilaterals include the United Kingdom's Department for International Development (DFID), Germany's Corporation for International Cooperation (known by its German acronym GIZ), Australia's Department for Foreign Affairs and Trade (DFAT), and the Japan International Cooperation Agency (JICA).

Bilateral donor organizations can bring significant assets to a partnership. These include not just funding but also the knowledge and expertise derived from decades of work on challenging problems around the world as well as the prestige and influence associated with a powerful national government. Convening interested people and organizations to explore solutions to a problem is much easier when you have the backing of a bilateral donor organization.

However, working with bilateral donors also has its downsides. Because they manage taxpayer money, bilateral agencies typically have very high levels of accountability regarding how they use their budgets. Consequently, they often have difficulty moving quickly, and the reporting requirements they place on organizations receiving aid can be burdensome. What's more, some countries impose restrictions on the ability of agencies to partner with companies headquartered in another country. This so-called *source of origin* issue can be a limiting factor in cross-sector partnerships. For example, as a general rule, JICA collaborates most closely with Japanese companies and organizations. The U.S. Congress also mandates that much U.S. foreign assistance be channeled through American contractors and NGOs.

The fact that bilateral donor agencies rely on contractors and NGOs to do the on-the-ground work as technical assistance providers and implementers can sometimes present another challenge. Donor agreements with contractors and NGOs can be very rigid, making it difficult to engage with them. Margaret Henry recalls a time when PepsiCo sought a partnership with a donor agency that seemed to have complementary objectives, only to run into unexpected roadblocks. "We were trying to plug into an existing USAID project," she says. "But they had their project, they had their goals, and they simply weren't interested in flexing."

Thus, the donor agency focus on accountability and process, while understandable, can be problematic. PepsiCo's Rob Meyers laments, "On the donor side, sometimes folks lose sight of the finish line. By contrast, in business, there has to be a result that we recognize as successful. There has to be a solution to a problem. A business can't have success defined as a bunch of activities—we need actual results."

Multilateral organizations. Multilateral organizations represent the interests of multiple governments on a particular topic or issue. For example, the United Nations sponsors a wide range of organizations focused on specific topics: The United Nations Children's Fund (UNICEF), the United Nations High Commissioner for Refugees (UNHCR), the United Nations Conference on Trade and development (UNCTAD), and many more. Outside of the UN system, there are also regional organizations like the Organization for Security and Cooperation in Europe (OSCE), the African Union (AU), and the Association of South East Asian Nations (ASEAN).

Multilateral organizations can bring significant legitimacy, convening power, and expertise to cross-sector partnerships. Their international scope can be an asset when you are tackling a problem that crosses national borders. However, they can be complicated to work with. Most are funded, directly or indirectly, by member governments, meaning that they have often have little funding of their own. Moreover, many of these organizations rely on making decisions through consensus across member states, which limits their ability to move quickly.

In addition, multilateral organizations may have a strong desire to avoid the appearance of being politically or financially linked with private partners. As a director of sustainability at a giant global consumer goods company observes, "When you work with partners like the UN that want to be appear to be neutral, it is a little difficult. They may not want to be too closely associated with your brand, but the reason we partner with them is that we want their legitimacy." Navigating this clash of values can be diplomatically challenging.

Host government agencies. Government agencies are critical partners in many partnerships. They can provide legitimacy, policy guidance, local expertise, funding, and often a pathway for scaling a partnership at the local, regional, or national levels. For all these reasons, host government agencies can be powerful partners.

However, they can also be major impediments to a partnership's success. They may be slow-moving and bureaucratic in their decision-making style, and they may impose onerous re-

porting requirements similar to those demanded by bilateral donor agencies. They can also be affected by domestic political cur-
rents—for example, when two or more ministries or departments are involved in a single partnership, they may have
conflicting goals and policy views that make collaboration complicated. Therefore, it's critical that you think through whether
you need a government partner and, if so, how you can best work
with them to maximize your chance of success.

In the Medtronic Labs case, host government agencies
made up the bulk of the health care delivery system in both
Kenya and Ghana. Therefore, Chemu understood very early on
that Medtronic would have to partner closely with a variety of
government players at different levels. This would demand patience and flexibility—for example, the willingness to deal with a
shifting cast of collaborators when government personnel
changes occurred. "Anything you do with the public sector takes
time," Chemu warns. When partnering with a government office
is essential, embark on the journey with realistic expectations.

Non-governmental organizations (NGOs). NGOs are mis-
sion-driven organizations, typically funded by grants from foundations or donor agencies or by private donations. They can
range enormously in size from small, neighborhood-based,
community-based, or faith-based organizations to multibillion-
dollar behemoths like the World Wildlife Fund or Save the Children.

NGOs generally fall into one of two broad categories: *advocacy NGOs* and *operational NGOs*. Advocacy NGOs typically
work to push for changes in government and corporate policies
in relation to particular cause—the environment, human rights,
education, health care, and so on. For example, Greenpeace is
an example of an environmental advocacy NGO, while the

American Civil Liberties Union is a human rights advocacy NGO. Pepsico's Simon Lowden observes, "I think advocacy NGOs help inform and shape what we do. We will never be in one-hundred-percent alignment with Greenpeace or others—nor should we, nor should they be one-hundrd-percent aligned with us. But we have to be informed about each other."

By contrast, operational NGOs focus on executing projects and programs that advance their mission. Save the Children is an example of an operational NGO that works to advance the welfare of children around the world. Again, Simon Lowden: "NGOs can provide catalytic platforms through which we can stimulate economic interest in doing things in a better way. NGOs bring expertise, they bring networks, and sometimes they bring funding—all of which is valuable."

The distinction between advocacy and operational NGOs is not hard and fast; it is more of a continuum, with some NGOs focused more advocacy, while others are more focused operationally.

NGOs can bring a range of assets to a partnership. Some have strong public reputations that can lend credibility to a project. In addition, NGOs often serve as third-party managers, backbone organizations, or secretariats for multi-stakeholder and collective impact initiatives. For example, in chapter three, we described the Platform for Accelerating the Circular Economy (PACE). The World Resources Institute (WRI), a Washington, D.C.-based NGO, serves as the backbone organization for PACE.

Because most NGOs rely on funding from donations, grants, membership dues, and other sources in order to fund their work, much as for-profit businesses need revenue to fuel their operations, they may be reluctant to join a partnership that could drain their resources. NGOs also tend to be highly mission-focused, which means that your best chance of engaging successfully will be with an NGO whose overarching mission is closely aligned with your problem-solving objective.

Private foundations. Private foundations typically make grants to other charitable organizations. There are more than 40,000 private foundations in the United States alone, as well as tens of thousands in other countries. They range from small, family-run foundations to large global players like the Bill & Melinda Gates and Rockefeller Foundations. In addition to the funding they provide, well-run foundations with experience in a particular problem area can bring significant expertise to a partnership. What's more, because foundation funding comes from private sources, foundations can often shoulder more financial risk than donor agencies.

Foundations can be great partners, but they also have some limitations. Only the very largest foundations have extensive reach internationally; others may have limited experience with working internationally or in low-resource environments. Many have opaque decision-making processes that can be frustrating for partners to deal with.

Precompetitive Partnering: The World Cocoa Foundation Example

Sometimes, the best potential partner is not from another sector. Sometimes the best partner is a firm with which you compete, especially if you are seeking to solve a problem that is impacting the entire industry. In such a case, competing industry players may form a precompetitive partnership to develop shared approaches and solutions that benefit the industry as a whole as well as other stakeholders.

The cocoa industry is facing a host of sustainability challenges involving issues such as deforestation, child labor, and declining farmer livelihoods. Many of these issues impact and are influenced by the entire industry, including cocoa producers, cocoa processors, and confectionary brands that market products containing cocoa to consumers.

To address these challenges, in 2001, leading players from the cocoa industry formed the World Cocoa Foundation (WCF). Members include all of the major confectionary brands as well as buyers and processors, representing about 85 percent of the global cocoa trade—Nestlé, Mars, Hershey, Olam, Cargill, and so on. WCF in turn partners with a host of donor agencies and foundations, including USAID and the Gates Foundation, tackling industry-wide problems at the systems level, with companies making individual commitments that align with shared WCF objectives. Because it represents so much buying power within the industry, WCF is able to engage with host governments to solve policy issues impacting sustainability, such as land tenure policies. In the words of Paul Macek, the WCF's vice president of programs, "These issues require collective effort even though we are strong competitors in the marketplace."

WCF represents an example of precompetitive partnering, in which companies in the same industry pool assets and capabilities to tackle common problems, then proceed to compete in the marketplace as usual. As you might imagine, precompetitive partnering must be managed carefully to avoid triggering concerns regarding collusion and antitrust violations among regulators and watchdog groups.

The cocoa industry is not alone in developing these sort of precompetitive partnerships. Coca-Cola and PepsiCo—two legendarily fierce competitors—are partnering around plastics and the circular economy. According to PepsiCo's Simon Lowden, "There is a time for competition and there is a time for precompetition. There is a new model emerging where you will see Coca-Cola and PepsiCo working together to provide industry solutions." What's more, this collaboration is supported at the highest levels inside the respective companies: "Ramon and James [the CEOs of PepsiCo and Coca-Cola] have been on the stage together," Simon observes. "What they talk about is becoming more and more similar on circularity."

Using Partner Profiles to Identify High-Potential Partners

As you identify potential partners, you may find it useful to compile *partner profiles*. These are simple charts tracking basic information about the organizations you consider potential partners. Figure 5-2 offers a set of questions you can use to gather the data needed for your partner profiles.

Figure 5-2: Partner Profile Questions

Organization Description	• What is the organization's purpose? • What does it need to accomplish? • What problems is it trying to solve? • What needs is it trying to satisfy?
Organizational Goals	• What does the organization dream about accomplishing? • How does it measure success? • What would make its job easier?
Organizational Challenges and Risks	• What risks does the organization fear? • What keeps its leaders awake at night? • What are the main difficulties and challenges they face?
Organizational Resources	• What non-financial or in-kind resources does the organization bring to the table? • Does it bring financial resources as well?

Answering these questions requires some research. Helpful resources include organization websites, government portals, and industry and trade association websites. You can also learn a lot about the activities, policies, goals, and challenges your potential partners are involved with by conducting a Google search for recent press coverage as well as a social media scan. You may also find it helpful to create a partner profile of your own organization, using the same set of questions. This exercise can help to ensure that you and your team are clear on why you want to partner and what you are bringing to the table.

As you work on compiling information about potential partners, remember that the resources needed for a successful partnership include much more than money. While funding can be critically important, it is often not the most significant value a partner can bring. A donor agency may have deep ties to civil society and government partners based on preexisting relationships of a kind that might take your company years to build. A foundation may have deep expertise in designing and successfully implementing programs. A government agency may have the power to convene a high-level meeting with important power brokers. So when thinking about resources, be sure to think beyond cash!

Creating and studying partner profiles can help you prioritize those potential partners who bring capabilities of all kinds that may be needed to tackle the problem. It can also help you develop a basic understanding of how a potential partner might view the problem you face.

Your goal at this stage is to identify *high-potential partners.* What makes for a high-potential partner? The answer may vary from one problem to another, but in general a high-potential partner:

o Sees the problem to be solved—or at least one dimension of the problem—as a high-priority issue for their organization

o Has resources—funding, technology, convening power, expertise, and so on—that complement the resources your own organization can bring to the table

o Is prepared to act; has a sense of urgency and a willingness to take concrete steps to tackle the problem

At PepsiCo, Margaret Henry and her team started with an initial list of about three dozen organizations, including some of PepsiCo's competitors, that appeared to be working on the problem of sustainable agricultural yields, or were otherwise interested in the issue of empowering women in agriculture in developing countries like India. Then they whittled down the list to focus on partners with a high level of engagement and readiness to act.

Among the characteristics PepsiCo looked for were the sense that agriculture supply chains represented a key business industry; a view of India as an important growth market; and what Margaret calls "local capacity on the ground to execute."

By prioritizing in this way, you can keep the number of likely partners to a manageable number. PepsiCo, for example, reduced its original list of possible partners to just six whom they regarded as high-potential. Keep in mind, however, that the partner profiles you've created are based on your assumptions; they are still hypothetical at this point.

Engaging Potential Partners

Now you need to test your assumptions by engaging directly with high-potential partners. The goal is to find organizations that will be powerful collaborators with you in tackling the problem you face while creating business value. Part of your quest is to find organizations whose leaders are ready to embrace your vision of a possible solution to the problem. For example, when PepsiCo prepared to begin meeting with possible partners, it was very clear about what it hoped to accomplish. As summarized by Margaret Henry, "We set out to make a business case as well as a social case for doing women's economic empowerment within our supply chains and for linking up that vision with our buyers." In the engagement process, you'll share your vision and gauge the responses of the people you hope to work with.

As you begin this step, Margaret Henry recommends doing some prep work with your team. "Before we meet with a donor or NGO," she says, "I like to have my staff document what they think they are going to hear and see in the meeting. Then I ask them to set those assumptions aside and go into the meeting with open minds. Later, we'll debrief so we can check and sometimes actively challenge our preexisting assumptions."

Here are a few additional pointers to keep in mind as you prepare to engage with potential partners.

Be willing to meet to get a meeting. It can be hard to glean from the outside who is the right person to meet with in a potential partner organization. After all, no two organizations are alike, and donor agencies, government ministries, and NGOs often use job titles that are unfamiliar in the world of business: *program officer, chief of party, mission director, capacity building advisor,* and so on. What's more, as PepsiCo's Rob Meyers observes, "When you have a business person and a donor person together for the first time, they are often talking completely different languages." So don't be surprised if your first engagement meeting seems unproductive. Be patient and persistent. If a partnership is meant to happen, you will soon find your way to the right person or group within the partner organization.

It's an exploration, not a sales pitch. One mistake business professionals often make is to approach an initial meeting with the goal of "selling" the potential partner on the benefits of a partnership. This is likely to backfire. Many professionals in the government and nonprofit world dislike sales pitches and are likely to be turned off by them. Instead, approach the engagement meeting as an exploration, seeking to understand the organization, its interests, challenges, and goals. This will help you start the relationship off on the right foot.

Ask open-ended questions. Partnerships are about relationships, which are built on trust and mutual understanding. To launch the process of building such a relationship, come to the discussion with three or four open-ended questions—not questions that can be answered with a simple yes or no—that you are really interested in learning about. This approach can help turn the meeting into a true conversation rather than an interview or survey.

Give and get. Everyone's time is precious, and it's important to respect that fact. One way of demonstrating respect for a potential partner's time is to practice *give and get.* In return for the time your counterpart gives to the meeting, be ready to offer up something of modest value in return—a report your company has produced, an introduction to someone influential in your field, an advance preview of an initiative you're launching, or anything else you are free to give that your potential partner may find of interest.

Practice the 30/70 rule. Aim to spend only about 30 percent of the time during the meeting speaking. Devote the other 70 percent to giving the other party an opportunity to explain their organization.

Ask who else cares. At an appropriate moment in the conversation, ask who else might be interested in the problem you are trying to solve. There may be others inside the organization or in other organizations that could be good potential partners.

Through these engagement meetings, you can refine your list of high-potential partners, gradually zeroing in on a few organizations that share your interest in solving the problem and have resources to offer toward a solution.

Creating and Iterating a Partnership Concept

Once you have some clarity around the problem to be solved and a list of high-potential partners, it is time to start developing a *partnership concept.* This is a brief statement that summarizes the problem, your possible solution, and the ways in which a partnership may successfully implement the solution. In the course of your engagement meetings with high-potential partners, you can use the partnership concept as a way of launching the discussion and gauging their interest. You'll likely find yourself revising, refining, and clarifying the partnership concept as time passes, partly in response to ideas and insights offers by your potential partners.

To help you get started on drafting your partnership concept, here are some questions to consider:

- o *Why?* Why are we considering a partnership? What is the shared problem that needs to be solved?
- o *Who?* Who are the potential partners that can bring the greatest value to solving the problem?
- o *What?* What are the resources—funding, expertise, convening power, technology, networks, and so on—that each partner could bring to the partnership?
- o *How?* What activities need to be undertaken to solve the problem?
- o *Where?* Is there a definable geographic region in which our activities will occur?
- o *So what?* What are some potential results of the partnership, in terms of business value or environmental or social impacts?
- o *What must be true?* What critical assumptions must hold true for a partnership to succeed?

Your partnership statement doesn't need to go into detail; just a summary sentence or a short paragraph will suffice. For example, the partnership concept for the PepsiCo project might have been a sentence like this one:

By empowering women farmers with new skills, access to finance, and technical support, the partnership among PepsiCo, NGOs, and donor agencies will increase yields and incomes in farming communities in northern India.

Similarly, the Medtronic project might have been summarized in this way:

By providing an integrated, end-to-end solution for hypertension and diabetes care, Medtronic, along with its government and NGO partners, can reduce the chronic disease burden experienced by patients, health care providers, and the health care system in Ghana and Kenya.

With a clear, well-defined partnership concept developed, you are now in a position to go deep with your high-potential partners in order to secure commitments and structure your partnership.

6

Internal Alignment and Buy-in

- o Why internal alignment is crucial to the success of cross-sector partnerships
- o The seven key elements of internal buy-in, and how to achieve them

Dateline: South Africa. Internal alignment is a challenge for all organizations, including businesses, NGOs, and government agencies. It is a particular challenge in the context of cross-sector partnerships, as my experience with a leading donor agency in South Africa taught me.

In 2005, shortly after founding the company that would become Resonance, I got a plum assignment: to help a major donor agency convene a meeting of for-profit companies in South Africa with the goal of forging a number of partnerships. For me, this was an amazing opportunity. I had spent the first decade of my career working in the former Soviet Union, and I was eager to branch out to different parts of the world. So this chance to work on partnerships in South Africa was a great opportunity.

After a journey of more than thirty hours, I arrived at the client's offices in Pretoria, South Africa, feeling exhausted yet exhilarated. I met with the head of the donor agency's local office, and we discussed her interest in collaborating with the private sector in areas ranging from public health to municipal financing of housing projects. I then had one-on-one meetings with the directors in charge of different parts of the donor's portfolio—governance, environment, education, and so on. Roughly 85 percent of the agency's budget in South Africa was dedicated to fighting the HIV/AIDS epidemic, then at its height, so I knew the health team would be critical to the success of my engagement.

When the time came for my meeting with health office director—I'll call him Richard—he invited me into his office and closed the door. "I understand you are here to help us build partnerships and alliances with corporations," he said. "Is that right?"

"Yes."

"I want to be very clear with you," Richard said. "I joined this agency precisely because I did *not* want to work with private sector companies. Corporations raped this continent for decades. I am here to help the people of South Africa, not the shareholders of some multinational company. We have a budget of more than a hundred million dollars per year, and we cannot spend it fast enough. So I do not need dirty corporate money. I think what you are trying to do is wrong and a waste of our time. The health team will not be involved or support your work."

Speech concluded, he sat back and folded his arms.

I sat there, silent. Without the health team, the vast bulk of the agency's work in South Africa would be excluded from the convening. Unless I could find a way to change Richard's attitude, the whole engagement would be a disaster.

It was one hell of a first day.

Seven Steps in Building Internal Alignment and Buy-In

My encounter with the Richard was far from unique. Over the years, I've seen many promising partnerships collapse because of internal conflicts at one or more of the partners. In fact, I would argue that lack of internal alignment is the *number one* reason partnerships fail, either while they are being built or, even worse, during implementation.

In a sense, it's understandable that cross-sector partnerships often fail to win universal buy-in among the team members of partner organizations. For most organizations, such partnerships are new and unfamiliar, and new approaches of any kind are often met with concern, skepticism, and sometimes outright hostility. Furthermore, cross-sector partnerships usually involve organizations with very different goals, hierarchies, and cultures, so there are any number of reasons why particular stakeholders within a company might oppose a partnership—financial, procedural, even ideological. But internal alignment is the crucial bedrock upon which all successful partnerships are built. If one partner has an internal alignment problem, the whole partnership can easily collapse.

There is no single formula to forging internal alignment, since every company and organization is different. However, there are some general principles that you can apply to foster buy-in and alignment. In this chapter, we'll share insights from partnership champions from very different organizations regarding the challenges of building and maintaining internal alignment as well as the techniques they use to generate buy-in.

There are seven key steps in building and maintaining internal buy-in when forging and managing a partnership.

1. Stakeholder Mapping—Getting the Lay of the Land
2. Making Allies and Educating Skeptics
3. Framing the Business Case
4. Aligning with Company Purpose
5. Aligning Headquarters Imperatives with On-the-Ground Realities
6. Coordinating Internal Communications
7. Obtaining Executive Sponsorship

Let's consider what's involved in each of these seven steps.

Step 1: Stakeholder Mapping— Getting the Lay of the Land

When you are leading an organization through the initial stages of building a cross-sector partnership, devote some time to exploring the internal landscape. Start by figuring out which people, groups, or business units within your company will play a role in deciding whether the partnership moves forward. Who could be potential champions? Who is likely to have concerns, doubts, or fears about the partnership? Who could throw up roadblocks in the way of a partnership agreement or its implementation?

If you are part of a large multinational company, you may discover that a wide range of departments is likely to be involved in planning—or preventing—a partnership. The players may include:

- o Sustainability/Corporate social responsibility (CSR)
- o Corporate affairs/Government affairs/Communications
- o Sourcing/Supply chain management
- o Operations
- o Corporate foundation
- o Marketing
- o Human Resources
- o Legal/Corporate counsel
- o Finance

o Country-level subsidiaries or business units

Take time to list the individuals or business units in your company that may have a stake in a potential partnership. Brainstorm with a couple of colleagues if necessary. Once you have the internal stakeholders identified, try to prioritize those who are most important. You can use a simple influence/interest matrix to map the various stakeholders (Figure 6-1 shows the parameters of such a matrix).

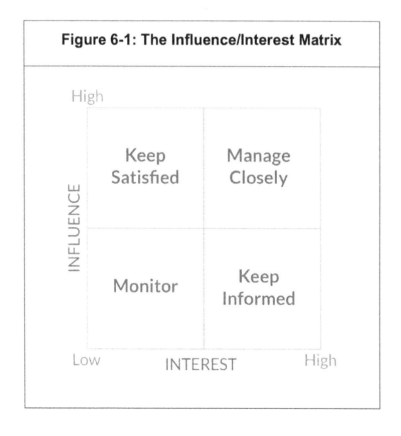

Figure 6-1: The Influence/Interest Matrix

Stakeholders in the upper right-hand quadrant of the influence/interest matrix have both a high degree of influence over and interest in the potential partnership. For obvious reasons, this group deserves the highest priority. Those in the upper left quadrant (high influence/low interest) need to be kept satisfied, but they will not require as much active engagement. Those in the lower right quadrant (low-influence/high interest) need to be kept informed, but they will not require significant consultation. Stakeholders in the lower left quadrant will probably play little role in the partnership saga.

The next step is to analyze the interests and potential concerns of your high-priority stakeholders. Your job is to discover how the idea of a cross-sector partnership looks to these stakeholders, based on their organizational interests, goals, challenges, and needs. In the words of Amanda Gardiner, formerly director of global sustainability and social innovation at Pearson, the world's largest educational publisher, "You need to meet people where they are. Understand your key internal stakeholders and what they need—and try to deliver it."

For example, professionals in the corporate affairs department may be primarily concerned about the reputational risks of a partnership. Members of the legal team will likely be focused on any potential legal liabilities that could emerge from the partnership. Leaders of a local business subsidiary may worry most about whether their time and energy bandwidth will be sufficient to support a partnership while still meeting their other business targets. Supply chain managers may be concerned about disruptions to their ability to keep a steady stream of resources flowing to the operational units of the company. As you hear from individuals in the various company departments, maintain a running list of the challenges raised, so that you can track them and address them in the course of building the partnership.

Step 2: Making Allies and Educating Skeptics

Now it's time to engage your internal stakeholders. Talk with them about their major concerns or interests regarding the potential partnership. In some cases, you may be able to assure your stakeholders that the partnership will not generate any new or insoluble problems for them. In other cases, you may realize that your stakeholders have valid concerns that need to be addressed by carefully designing aspects of the partnership to avoid needless risks or complications.

PepsiCo's Rob Meyers has had experience with the process of engaging internal stakeholders. He lists some of the questions he has had to explore while discussing partnerships issues with his colleagues at PepsiCo: "What are our business priorities in India? What's the growth agenda there? What are our business objectives? What are the constraints we face? What are the major factors we worry about?" Rob goes on to explain how he responds to such questions. "We really try to understand those priorities, and then align our partnerships to support the business. Our Sustainable Farming Program has been successful because we have demonstrated that sustainable agriculture meets business priorities and overcomes constraints."

As you spend time with internal stakeholders, you may discover some who can serve as champions of the partnership—internal allies who see the value of cross-sector collaboration and are willing to help you explain the advantages to others. Keep these people fully informed, and consider calling on them to help you win over skeptics.

Converting doubters is a process that requires both learning and educating. You need to understand both the needs of allies and the concerns of skeptics. In turn, you need to educate both allies and skeptics to understand the nature of the problem you are trying to solve, why a cross-sector partnership is the right approach, and the mutual benefits to be derived from a successful partnership. Don't short-circuit this job. It's a crucial one that will reward the time and energy you invest in it.

Step 3: Framing the Business Case

In some companies, the thought of partnering with an NGO or a government agency may seem very unorthodox. After all, most successful companies are successful because they maintain a tight focus on their customers and the products and services they provide to them. Partnering with an NGO or a government agency may seem like a waste of time to some. Others, who are used to thinking of NGOs and government agencies as adversaries rather than partners, may worry that the NGO will attack their reputation if the NGO learns that the company is doing anything wrong. Furthermore, a partnership is a time-intensive undertaking; every moment spent on a partnership is a moment that cannot be devoted to some other task. As Pearson's Amanda Gardiner notes, "In companies you need to do, do and deliver, in three-month timeframes. That can be hard in the context of a partnership."

For all these reasons, it's important to get clear, very early in the process, about the business case for the partnership. You'll need to list and justify the business benefits the company can expect from a successful partnership. The goal is to show your profit-oriented colleagues that a cross-sector partnership is not just a matter of altruism; it is also a powerful tool for improving the long-term health and success of your company.

There are a number of examples of possible business benefits, many of which may apply to the partnership you are seeking to launch. A successful cross-sector partnership can enable a participating company to:

- o Access new markets or customers
- o Source more, better, or less-costly materials
- o Increase productivity
- o Reduce customer or supplier churn
- o Increase operating efficiency
- o Develop and test new business models
- o Reduce risk and maintain social license to operate
- o Attract or retain top-flight talent

Most companies run on quantitative metrics. Therefore, try to use your company's own metrics when making the case for the value of a partnership. Arguments like the following, which include specific quantitative objectives, are likely to be more persuasive than vague, non-quantitative promises.

- o "Through the partnership, we will be able to reach up to 250,000 new customers in peri-urban neighborhoods around Lagos."
- o "The partnership can help us reduce our input costs by 20 percent over the next two years."
- o "Thanks to the partnership, we expect to increase the capacity of our cold chain storage system by 22 percent."

o "We expect to reduce employee turnover by nine percent due to the impact of the partnership."

PepsiCo's Rob Meyers emphasizes this point:

> We communicate [internally] as quantitatively as possible where the business is receiving value. Where we can measure a decrease in grower turnover, where we can measure an increase in yield, where we can measure improved productivity, more efficiency, better quality, we measure these and communicate back to the business.
>
> We keep very close track of our partnerships in terms of dollars—both cash and in-kind—coming from the donors in support of the partnership . . . We are getting more value out of these partnerships than the cost of our team. It is really important to communicate the value you are bringing through these collaborations.

Partnerships can add value to the business in non-quantitative ways as well. Amanda Gardiner describes her experience at Pearson this way: "We made the [business] case by showing how the partnership would allow our product teams to apply their skills and expertise in ways that made an impact and also built knowledge inside the company on how to grow in global markets."

If you make the business case clear and compelling, you will find yourself in a much better position to justify the partnership and ensure that relevant business units remain engaged and supportive.

Step 4: Aligning with Company Purpose

In the 20th century era of shareholder capitalism, the idea of a "company purpose" beyond maximizing profits would have seemed quaint or perhaps even slightly subversive. As President Calvin Coolidge famously remarked, "The business of America is business."

No longer. Today, companies large and small increasingly find that having a purpose beyond mere profits is essential both for attracting and retaining the best talent and for engaging with customers. A growing body of research shows that companies that have a well-defined sense of purpose perform significantly better than their peers.

Because cross-sector partnerships create both business and social value, they are a powerful opportunity for a company to demonstrate its purpose to customers and employees alike. Thus, a key element in building internal buy-in for a partnership is aligning the partnership with company purpose. This creates an emotional element that helps bring employees and managers on board.

If your company has done a good job of defining and articulating its purpose, it will facilitate the task of aligning your partnership with that purpose. A compelling purpose statement clearly articulates the purpose for a company's existence and the value it brings to the world. However, relatively few companies have clear purpose statements. If your company lacks such a statement, try reviewing recent speeches, presentations, or interviews featuring the CEO or other top company leaders. You may also want to brainstorm with fellow employees about how their work ignites their passions.

Try to identify the values that give larger meaning to the operations of your company; then seek ways to align the partnership with those values. Look for opportunities to highlight that alignment as you prepare internal materials about the partnership: presentations, reports, concept notes, business plans, and so on. Doing so will make it easier for your fellow employees and managers to see how the partnership adds value to the company, not only in financial terms but also in terms of the larger organizational purpose.

Step 5: Aligning Headquarters Imperatives with On-the-Ground Realities

Many cross-sector partnerships are forged and negotiated between partners at the headquarters level, then must be operationalized in frontier markets in Africa, Asia, or Latin America. This top-down approach to partnerships often leads to tensions within companies between the HQ team and the in-country business unit.

In some cases, the HQ staff understanding of the in-country operating context is limited. As a result, the partnership gets designed in a way that does not fully solve the problem it aims to address. In other cases, in-country business units are expected to operationalize and support a partnership that may not fully align with the key performance indicators (KPIs) and budget resources specified in their operating plans. Consequently, their ability to act may be limited. As one sustainability director for a global consumer goods giant notes, "There is sometimes a misfit in terms of who has the power and who makes the decisions regarding the partnership. At the local level, your business unit may want to work with a different partner or do something else entirely."

PepsiCo's Rob Meyers describes the dynamic this way: "In a lot of corporate cultures, you have a wall. On one side, you have the corporate function, and on the other side, you have the business. The corporate side tosses things over the wall, and the business needs to respond." This kind of dissonance between HQ and in-country business units can cause partnerships to fail.

The lesson for would-be partnership builders is clear: If you are in HQ and negotiating a partnership, make sure you identify your in-country business unit as a key stakeholder and engage with them early and often. Make sure they understand the goals of the partnership and its importance to overall corporate objectives. Even more important, seek their advice regarding how the partnership should be developed and operationalized. This not only increases buy-in, but ensures that your partnership is designed with the local context and realities built in. This approach can greatly increase the partnership's chances for success.

"We try to remove that wall," Rob Meyers says. "We try to put the business on top."

Step 6: Coordinating Internal Communications

No one within a company likes to be surprised or caught off guard about a potentially high-profile initiative such as a cross-sector partnership. Therefore, frequent and clear communication with your internal stakeholders is essential. Here are some methods you can use to enhance your internal communications about the partnership.

Distribute weekly or monthly email updates on partnership-building progress. These can be simple bullet-point updates that let your stakeholders know about how you are achieving key milestones.

Hold regular stage-gate meetings. Stage-gating is the process by which a project is allowed to advance to its next stage of development after a *gated review* that ensures that everything is on track and aligned within the company. When negotiating partnerships for which there is significant internal skepticism or resistance, holding stage-gating meetings attended by all the key players can be helpful to ensure that you do not get too far out in front of your most important stakeholders. Stage-gating meetings also demonstrate forward progress and momentum, which can help to build enthusiasm and maintain internal buy-in. (More on stage-gating in chapter eight of this book.)

Convene a partnership team or cross-business-unit working group. A growing number of companies, including PepsiCo, Microsoft, and Unilever, have established teams focused on building and managing cross-sector partnerships. To be effective, these teams require the ability to work across business units in order to engage and leverage the capabilities of those units. The teams also help to ensure that people and groups throughout the company are keep informed about partnership developments. (More on partnership teams in chapter eleven of this book.)

Step 7: Obtaining Executive Sponsorship

In many companies, having high-level and even C-suite support proves to be a critical factor in driving internal alignment around a partnership. When the CEO is a committed supporter of cross-sector partnerships, others throughout the company are likely to fall in line as well.

Because every company has its own unique culture, value system, and processes, there is no one path to obtaining executive sponsorship. However, there are a few things you can do to better position the partnership to obtain such high-level support. These include looking for ways to get the partnership on the radar screen of senior executives; clearly and explicitly aligning the partnership's goals with high-priority C-suite initiatives; and creating opportunities for senior executives to participate in key partnership events—the ceremonial signing of a memo of understanding, press conferences, speaking engagements, ribbon-cuttings, VIP site visits, and so on.

On the other hand, don't make the mistake of elevating a potential partnership too early. PepsiCo's Margaret Henry warns, "Don't just let loose with your executives and get them so excited about external funds that you bring people in before you know how to translate ideas into action. If you do that, you will lose them."

Creative, Patient, Persistent: The Path to Alignment

In many companies, it is not possible to complete all seven steps in the alignment process. That's all right; not all seven steps may be necessary. It's up to you to determine which elements are the most critical for your organization and its culture. By being proactive about cultivating and maintaining buy-in and internal alignment, you can greatly reduce the headaches and roadblocks you'll encounter as you move forward with building a partnership.

Let's flash back to my South Africa experience. Following my initial, very discouraging meeting with Richard, the head of the agency's health team, I paused to take stock. I knew that I had executive-level sponsorship for the partnership concept from the head of the South Africa office, so, despite Richard's skepticism, he could not totally dismiss my efforts. But I still need to find a way to overcome his resistance.

I soon discovered that there were a couple of specialists on the health team who understood that the magnitude of the HIV/AIDS crisis required putting every option on the table. As a result, they were eager to explore partnering with the private sector. These specialists became my allies, and I made sure they were continually informed about my efforts.

I also began working to identify companies that were serious about tackling the HIV/AIDS crisis in South Africa. Given the magnitude of the pandemic and its impact on workforce health and absenteeism, there were a number of South African companies that were already investing heavily in combatting HIV/AIDS in their workforces and who were eager to partner with donors and NGOs to do more. With input from my allies on the health team, I identified two companies—DeBeers Group and Anglo Platinum—that appeared to be high-potential partners.

As a next step, I organized a panel discussion about the HIV/AIDS crisis that would include representatives from DeBeers and Anglo Platinum as well as a leader from the South African Business Coalition on HIV—along with Richard himself.

I was extremely nervous on the day of the conference, unsure as to how the panel discussion would play out. Would the company representatives say or do something that would torpedo the potential for a partnership before it had even been launched? Would Richard give vent to his hostility toward corporate businesses, making further discussion pointless?

My fears proved to be unfounded. The leaders from De-Beers and Anglo Platinum had a very sophisticated understanding of HIV/AIDS and its devastating human impact. Richard was clearly impressed by their presentations and by the health care programs they'd developed and implemented for their workforce and the surrounding communities. The panel discussion was extremely rich and surfaced a number of areas in which the donor agency and the companies could collaborate.

When the panel ended, Richard pulled me aside. "We should be working with these companies!" he told me.

It wasn't quite a "Thank you," but I was happy to take it.

7

Closing the Deal

- o The Valley of Partnership Death
- o Understanding and negotiating with partners
- o Structuring a cross-sector partnership
- o Making decisions about partnership governance and management
- o Negotiating a partnership agreement

Dateline: Syria: Negotiating and designing a partnership is never easy. It may require tremendous perseverance to overcome differences in institutional cultures and ways of operating. It may also require a high degree of comfort with ambiguity as prospective partners iterate towards a shared understanding of the problem, a shared understanding of the solution, and a shared understanding of how to get there.

Amanda Gardiner knows these issues well from her time at the education company Pearson, where she was charged with building cross-sector partnerships. "Let's face it," she says, "many companies initially pursue social impact partnerships for brand-enhancement purposes, before evolving into more transformative relationships. That's just where Pearson was at the time."

Founded as a construction company in the United Kingdom in the 1840s, Pearson got into publishing in the 1920s, and for decades it was known for its textbooks. However, as Amazon increasingly disrupted the textbook market, the company pivoted its strategy to become "the world's learning company." It was natural for Pearson to have an interest in helping to create partnerships aimed at improving the educational opportunities available to less-fortunate children in the developing world. With a deep background at the United Nations and her direct, no-nonsense style, Amanda was uniquely qualified to help Pearson navigate this challenging terrain.

Pearson's first foray into the world of cross-sector partnerships emerged from a chance encounter. The Pearson CEO met the CEO of Save the Children UK at a conference. According to

Amanda, "They met, and it clicked. Both realized they were focused on positive change for children and young people, so they decided to find a way to collaborate." With little more than that to go on, it fell to Amanda, on her first day in her new role at Pearson, to work with the staff of Save the Children UK to figure out what the two organizations might do together.Getting to a partnership agreement was not easy. Following an initial meeting between the two teams, it took several months for Save the Children to draft a partnership concept paper. "When it arrived, it was all wrong," Amanda recalls. "Rather than describing a sustainable new project, we would basically be funding their existing work. That is not what Pearson was hoping to do." Save the Children UK appeared to be ignoring Pearson's considerable expertise in education and educational technologies, viewing the company purely as a source of money.

Amanda then decided to take a different tack. Working with her counterpart from Save the Children UK, Amanda brought stakeholders together from across both organizations into working groups to try to align around a shared objective. The working groups developed ideas over the period of two months, looking at three or four geographies where the two could work together. It was challenging for both sides, featuring an extended debate about possible directions. "The process was pretty painful," Amanda says.

At the time, the Syrian civil war was in its most devastating phase, causing millions of Syrians to flee their country as refugees. With more than 2.8 million children out of school because of the conflict, an entire generation of young Syrians was at risk of not being educated. The two organizations were attracted by the idea of partnering to help address the educational needs of

Syrian refugees, but it took them time to figure out where and how this could be done.

Through the working group process, the partners eventually agreed on a shared commitment to deliver high-quality education to Syrian refugee children in Jordan, with enough of the key details specified so that the partners could be comfortable moving forward on the project together. They then spent months working to define a shared vision of success as well as the resources that each partner could bring to the partnership.

Such travails are not unusual. Getting a corporation and an NGO or a government agency to agree on anything can very challenging, in part because organizations from these different sectors have widely differing worldviews, organizational cultures, and incentive structures.

I faced similar challenges when my team sought to forge a partnership to bring broadband to rural communities in Sri Lanka. In 2006, the country was in the midst of a tragic conflict. The world's longest-running civil war, between the Sri Lankan government and the rebel group known as the Tamil Tigers, had already resulted in tens of thousands of deaths, hundreds of thousands of refugees, and years of economic stagnation. Now the war was escalating from a low simmer to a steady boil after a new nationalist government had come to power with the mandate to win the fight once and for all.

Despite this backdrop of warfare, our efforts to build a partnership were starting to get some traction. We had met with a large number of potential partners—companies, government agencies, and NGOs—and identified a few that appeared to have the motivation and resources to bring the partnership to life. But we needed to move from talk to real commitment and from there to action.

The Valley of Partnership Death

In the world of startup businesses, there's a familiar phenomenon known as the Valley of Death. It's the time period when a firm goes cash-flow negative as it develops and refines its product, expands its team, invests in office space and equipment, and incurs other expenses without commensurate income. The Valley of Death is the time when most startups fail.

Partnerships, too, face a Valley of Death. It is the period after you have identified and engaged with potential partners. Interest appears strong, and you seem to be riding high. The challenge comes in converting that interest into real commitment and then into a partnership agreement. This journey can be long and arduous, often taking six months or more. Some promising partners may turn out not to be seriously interested. Others sit on the sidelines, waiting for others to take the lead. This is the phase where many promising partnerships lose momentum and die (Figure 7-1).

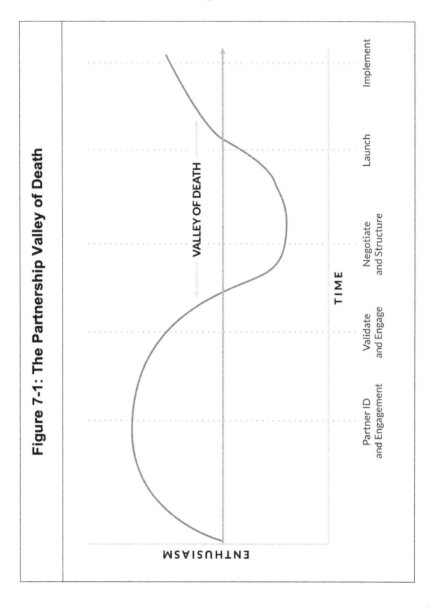

Figure 7-1: The Partnership Valley of Death

As illustrated by Amanda's experience with Save the Children as well as my experience in Sri Lanka, successfully traversing the Valley of Partnership Death can be difficult. Building and structuring a strong partnership has several challenging dimensions, including understanding partner incentives and constraints, securing commitments, creating a shared vision of success, and negotiating the details of a partnership agreement. Let's consider these one by one.

Understanding Partner Incentives and Constraints

As you begin to negotiate and structure your partnership, it is critical that you develop an understanding of the realities facing your partners. For business professionals who have spent their careers in the corporate world, the world of NGOs, philanthropic foundations, government agencies, and other non-business organizations can seem strange and counterintuitive, because their underlying incentive structures are fundamentally different. In particular, there are several features regarding the incentive structures of NGOs and donor agencies that surprise many business professionals.

Process often dominates. Because they are stewards of taxpayer funds, many donor agencies and multilateral organizations place a greater emphasis on getting the process right than most businesses. If you work for a donor agency, you are much more likely to be fired for not following proper procedure than for managing an unsuccessful program. Thus, if you are a business professional trying to forge a partnership with a donor agency, there may be times when it seems your partner counterpart is inordinately focused on getting approvals and documentation in place. Be patient: This is the nature of the game you are playing, and the rules must be followed, even if they are sometimes frustrating.

The mission can sometimes get in the way of the partnership. Employees at most donor agencies and NGOs are highly focused on delivering on their organizational mission. In general, this is a very good thing. But sometimes the focus on mission can lead to tunnel vision. For example, a donor agency focused on poverty may tend to ignore environmental considerations related to a project, while a health-oriented NGO may not understand how issues related to primary education may impact a health-centered program.

Rigidly earmarked funding can limit the freedom of donor agencies and NGOs. Donor agencies and NGOs often face tight restrictions on how they can use their funding. For example, the U.S. Congress frequently earmarks USAID's budget for very specific purposes, such as working with victims of war, or restricts the agency's ability to work on issues in reproductive health. Funding agreements between a donor and their NGO or implementing partners may then create additional contractual restrictions. These limitations can make it difficult to flex on how they run programs and expend funds in the context of a cross-sector partnership.

NGOs and donors often have longer event horizons than for-profit businesses. Most businesses, especially publicly traded corporations, tend to look at the world in three-month increments; many use internal key performance indicators (KPIs) aligned with quarterly earnings objectives. By contrast, most donor-funded nonprofit programs take years to design, roll out, and manage. For example, it typically takes USAID six to eighteen months to design a large project and another nine to twelve months to procure it. If it is a five-year project, this means the end-to-end project cycle is nearly seven years—the equivalent of several lifetimes in the business world.

Form sometimes trumps substance. The employees at most government agencies and multilateral donors strive to keep their leaders happy by giving them lots of "announceables"—ribbon cuttings, press conferences, panels at high-profile events, and so on. (Businesses sometimes face similar pressures from their C-suite leaders.) As a result, donor agencies may seem to have a greater focus on the fanfare surrounding the launch of a partnership than on the underlying substance.

Money matters . . . a lot. Many business professionals have a rosy picture of the NGO community as a collection of do-gooders dedicated to saving the world and not terribly interested in money. The reality is that most NGO employees think about money continually, because they must. NGOs need to fundraise aggressively in a very competitive environment, often under pressure from boards that set fundraising targets for their CEOs. As a result, disillusioned business leaders often end up uttering complaints like this one from Amanda Gardiner: "When NGOs look at companies, they just see dollar signs. They don't try to understand the business, where it is going, and the nonfinancial resources it can bring to the partnership."

Of course, all of the descriptions we've just provided are generalizations that don't apply to every NGO, government, or donor agency. But the underlying principle is the same: When negotiating a partnership, it's important to try to uncover and understand the incentives and constraints facing your partners, no matter how different they may seem from the ones you face as a business professional.

Similarly, it is important that you try to articulate and explain your company's incentives and constraints, whether they're about showing progress each quarter or delivering results by the end of a fiscal year. By getting these incentives out on the table, preferably early in the process, partners can begin to design the partnership so that that it aligns and balances conflicting institutional incentives and constraints in a way that serves the underlying goals of the partnership.

Securing Commitment

The biggest challenge in negotiating a partnership is often transitioning from an expression of interest to an actual commitment—not a formal, written agreement but a clear, reasonably well-defined intention to partner around solving a shared problem. Here are a few methods you can use to move from talk to commitment.

- ○ *Shuttle diplomacy.* It can take a surprising amount of back and forth among partners to develop a partnership as organizations with very different structures, cultures, and incentives try to align towards a common goal. Shuttle diplomacy is the process by which you negotiate individually with each of the potential partners, developing the broad outlines of a partnership. Be prepared to invest time in this process. It may take several meetings to uncover what a partner seeks to achieve through collaboration. It may also take time for an organization's internal stakeholders to align around the idea of a partnership.

o *Convene to commit.* It may be necessary to bring potential partners together for a roundtable discussion to talk through the potential partnership. This kind of session can be structured to nudge participants either to commit or step back. A convene-to-commit session can be a bit of a high-stakes gamble: What if no one steps up? Therefore, it's critical to lay the groundwork in advance, meeting with the potential partners one on one and making sure that they understand the purpose of the convening. Ideally, you'll want to identify at least one partner willing to commit at the session, thus creating a bit of positive peer pressure on the others.

o *Creating a sense of urgency.* In today's fast-paced world, the urgent often takes precedence over the important. Thus, creating a sense of urgency—a deadline that must be met—can be a useful way to focus minds and attention. A high-profile event can be used to create a firm deadline for partners to announce their commitments. David McGinty of PACE, for example, suggests targeting "a point on the calendar—a Davos or G-7 event—where partners can be seen and celebrated for taking action."

While working to build our Sri Lanka partnership, we used the convene-to-commit strategy. In advance of a roundtable, hosted by the U.S. ambassador, among the executives of our high-potential partners, we had secured a significant commitment from one of the partners, Dialog Telekom. This convening helped us narrow our list of about ten potential partners to five partners who were truly committed.

Moving from talk to sincere commitment is never easy, especially in a cross-cultural context. In some cultures, potential partners may be reluctant to say no to your proposal, even if they have no genuine interest, while in others, where a high value is placed on consensus and inclusion, it can be challenging to identify a small number of truly committed partners. Pay attention to such cultural differences, and try to enlist the help of a local expert who can help you navigate them with sensitivity.

Structuring a Partnership: Creating a Shared Vision of Success

Thai Union's Darian McBain says, "The sign of a true partnership is that you are going to change something in the world together." Once you have secured real commitment from your partners, it is time to begin crafting a vision of success—a detailed description of how you intend to change something in the world.

Creating a shared vision of success has several components.

First, you need to strive to develop a shared understanding of the problem. NGOs, companies, and governments will typically look at a problem from very different perspectives. For example, environmental NGOs will look at an issue of seafood sustainability from the perspective of preserving the oceans; food companies will tend to look at it as a matter of ensuring continued supply while meeting consumer expectations regarding sustainability; and governments will look at the same issue as a question of policy and regulation. You need a problem statement that is sufficiently inclusive of all partner perspectives. Next, work to craft a clear definition of success. Partnerships, particularly large, multi-stakeholder partnerships, sometimes fall victim to defining success too broadly or amorphously. For example, a success indicator like "We will partner to end global poverty" may sound impressive in a press release, but it's too broad to provide specific guidance for partners to manage against. A better definition of success might be something like, "We will work to reduce the percentage of individuals living on less than $5 per day in our target country from 30 percent to fewer than 10 percent."

A powerful tool for helping companies, NGOs, and government agencies to find common ground is the UN Sustainable Development Goals (SDGs). This document provides a set of 17 well-understood and widely accepted goals, underpinned by more than 100 specific targets and indicators. For example, SDG 3, "Good health and well-being," includes target 3.1, "By 2030, reduce the global maternal mortality ratio to less than 70 per 100,000 live births," and two related indicators, "maternal mortality ratio," and "proportion of births attended by skilled health personnel." Targets and indicators like these can partnership members with clear, measurable goals that they can agree on and work towards.

If you are struggling to identify goals that you can agree to share with non-business partners, you may find some helpful ideas by consulting the SDGs. What's more, as PepsiCo's Margaret Henry suggests, the goals you develop with your partners do not need to be completely identical, just "complementary."

Spend time with your partners striving to agree on *first principles*. Partnerships live and die on trust. When there is mutual trust, a partnership can have the resilience to withstand unforeseen problems and challenges. When trust is lacking, partnerships often collapse in bickering and accusations. Therefore, it is critical that the partners align on a set of first principles defining how they will interact with each other as partners.

For example, one first principle that Margaret Henry considers important is as follows: "Each person in their respective entities deals with their own internal politics, while letting the other partners know when political issues may impact a timeline or financing." You may or may not want to adopt this principle for your own partnership; what matters is that you discuss such rules and come to a general agreement with your partners.

To ensure true alignment, you may need to take a deep dive into your partner's organizational strategy. Sometimes an understanding at a superficial level comes undone upon deeper inspection. A director of sustainability at a global consumer goods firm offers a deceptively simple example from a partnership project her company joined. "We aligned with a major donor agency around financial inclusion in Nigeria," she recalls, "but it turned out their strategy focused on the northern part of the country while we were focused on the south."

It's also important to clarify partner constraints. Every organization faces constraints of various kinds—financial, organizational, political. A donor agency may face significant constraints regarding how it can deploy taxpayer money due to public procurement requirements; an NGO may have to avoid specific kinds of policy entanglements in deference to the views of a major donor or board member. As PACE's David McGinty emphasizes, "Be honest about the fact that institutions have motivations that can inhibit or accelerate progress. Once you unpack them, you can have a real conversation about how to deal with them." Getting clear on partner constraints can enable you to avoid straying into any "no-go zones" that could threaten the survival of the partnership.

Next, define the activities, roles, and responsibilities that each partner will take on and the resources they will contribute. Draw up a list of the activities the partners will undertake together. Then evaluate the resources each partner will contribute against your shared vision of success. Are they sufficient? Are there obvious gaps in capabilities? It is important to dig deep to get a realistic picture of each partner's capabilities. As a sustainability director at a global consumer goods giant observes, "From a global level, you can align with partners very easily. But at the local level, it is more complicated. What assets does each partner actually have at the local level?" This sort of ground-level analysis may uncover weaknesses you need to address before you begin work.

Finally, consider possible worst-case scenarios. What happens if a partner fails to deliver? What happens if a partner quits the partnership? By thinking through adverse scenarios in advance, you can build mechanisms into the partnership to mitigate these risks.

As you're working to develop a shared vision for your partnership, consider drafting a *partnership concept paper*. This is a simple document that summarizes the main features of the partnership. It can be an extremely effective tool for developing the shared vision for success. When building our Sri Lanka partnership, we used a series of concept papers to capsulize and refine the partnership concept. We took the lead on drafting the papers, then circulated them among all the partners for input and feedback. Afterward, our team met individually with each of the partners to review the papers and refine them further. (You can find a sample partnership concept paper in Appendix A in this book.)

If your partnership is relatively large and complex partnerships, consider holding a *co-creation workshop*—a meeting in which the partners gather to hammer out important partnership details over a period of one or two days. A co-creation workshop can be a powerful tool for creating shared vision of success and building trust among the partners.

Building a shared vision for a partnership is not easy. It takes time and patience. However, it is critically important that partners become fully aligned and understand what is expected of each other.

Donor Agency Partnering Platforms

Over the last two decades, many bilateral and multilateral donor organizations have established specialized units to foster partnerships with the private sector. Recognizing that government bureaucracies can be difficult for companies to navigate, the donor organizations designed these platforms to make the partnering process quicker and easier. In addition, several have made funds available, typically on a matching basis with corporate contributions to a partnership. Here are a few examples.

The United Nations Global Compact. One of the oldest and best-established cross-sector partnership platforms, the UN Global Compact engages companies in partnerships to combat poverty, inequality, and climate change. It has worked with more than 9,000 companies worldwide on a range of UN projects and initiatives.

The USAID Global Development Alliances (GDA). Managed by USAID's Center for Transformational Partnerships, the GDA has become one of the most common ways for America's largest development agency to partner with the private sector. GDA provides resources on a 1:1 matching basis.

The Business Partnerships Platform. This program, operated by Australia's Department of Foreign Affairs and Trade (DFAT), is similar to the USAID GDA. It's designed to facilitate cross-sector partnerships in those regions where Australia has strong development or trade interests, especially Asia and the Pacific.

The Business Partnership Fund. The United Kingdom's Department for International Development has launched the Business Partnership Fund, which is designed to "support multinational companies to develop projects that generate commercial value whilst also improving the lives of the poor in developing countries."

The Swedish International Development Agency (SIDA). SIDA partners with a wide range of private-sector partners—companies, banks, investors, and so on—through an approach it refers to as "private sector collaboration." Partnerships are initiated through Sweden's embassies in the target countries.

These platforms often have dedicated staff who understand the complexities of cross-sector partnerships. Thus, they can be a useful source of information and ideas when you begin thinking about partnering with a bilateral or multilateral donor agency.

Partnership Negotiating Principles

Most of the negotiating we do in our business and professional lives is adversarial in some way. When you buy a car, your goal is to negotiate the lowest price, while the salesperson is trying to negotiate the highest price.

Negotiating a partnership is quite different. A partnership is about creating wins for all sides—hence Ed Martin's term *omniwin*. What's more, a partnership is rarely a one-time transaction; instead, it is an ongoing relationship that may last many years. Therefore, it's not a good tactic to push aggressively for the best deal possible for your company at the expense of your partner. Instead, your goal should be to try to maximize the win for all partners involved.

This is a goal that calls for deep understanding and empathy across organizational and sector barriers. The challenge may be intensified if you are negotiating across cultures. For example, you may work for a large for-profit company based in Europe or North America, while your counterpart may work for an NGO based in Africa or Latin America. The resulting differences in values, assumptions, and communication styles can be tricky to navigate if you do not address them proactively.

Here are some common-sense tips that can help you do a more effective job when negotiating partnership terms.

- ○ *Practice active listening.* Ask open-ended questions that encourage your partners to articulate their situations and their perspectives on the partnership. Paraphrase what you've heard both to test and to demonstrate your understanding.
- ○ *Strive for a fair process.* Humans are wired to value fairness. Therefore, take care to ensure that the negotiation process is perceived as a fair one. Avoid backing partners into corners or forcing an issue.

o *Use power with restraint.* The Harvard Project on Negotiation places a great deal of emphasis on leveraging power dynamics in negotiations, whether based on a strong negotiating position, the power of a title or role, or the sheer force of your personality. However, in a partnership negotiating, using your power can backfire. Therefore, use your power with restraint, keeping in mind that the power dynamics may shift one day, bringing a time when your partner has significant power over you. Play the long game.

o *Show curiosity.* Do some basic research into your counterpart's organization, their personal background, and the cultural setting in which they work. Ask questions to learn more, a gesture that is almost always welcomed. Doing a bit of homework and showing a willingness to learn can go a long way to instilling trust and encouraging transparency.

o *Show respect for differences.* Differences in cultural practices and values can become major obstacles if not handled with care. By showing respect for such differences, you can anticipate issues before they arise and prevent them from impeding the negotiation process.

o *Be aware of how others may perceive your culture.* Don't forget that your counterpart may have specific perceptions about your culture, both geographic and organizational, that may or may not be accurate. You can help to build trust by asking about such perceptions and addressing their validity.

Taking an intentional approach to the partnership negotiation process can help you get to yes more quickly while maximizing the win for all partners.

Partnership Governance

A key question to be answered in the negotiation process is how the partnership will be governed. How will decisions be made, and who will make them? Will all partners have an equal say? How will outside stakeholders be consulted? The following are some key considerations when designing partnership governance structures.

Balance equity and inclusion with the need to act. On the one hand, a cross-sector partnership needs to treat partners with fairness and inclusion, giving everyone a chance to participate in important decisions. On the other hand, the partnership will be faced with the practical need to make decisions and get things done in a timely fashion. The more partners involved in any decision, the more time it will take to make. Therefore, it is worth considering the extent to which partners need to be involved in specific aspects of governance, as well as the kinds of circumstances in which a streamlined governance structure may be most effective.

Balance transparency with confidentiality. Partners also need to strike a balance between the need to be transparent about information relevant to decision-making, particularly in regard to decisions that will impact outside stakeholders, and the need to protect some level of confidentiality regarding sensitive or proprietary matters.

Strive for simplicity. In setting up a partnership governance system, it is important to remember the KISS rule: "Keep it simple, stupid." Overly complex governance structures risk creating both inefficiency and a lack of transparency.

There are two common types of governance structures for partnerships.

- ○ *The governing committee or task force.* Comprising empowered representatives of each of the partners, this governing body meets regularly—typically monthly or quarterly—to review progress and to make major decisions regarding activities, budgets, policy modifications, and similar matters.
- ○ *Tiered governance.* While the idea of giving equal voice to all partners is appealing, it can create headaches if the relative participation of different partners varies significantly—for example, if the financial commitments of the partners are very different. One solution is to create an executive committee that includes a small group of highly committed partners, while less committed partners serve as members of a larger committee. Under this tiered governance system, the executive committee has the power to make the major decisions, while the larger committee keeps all participants informed and on track.

In Sri Lanka, we wound up using a tiered approach. Our core partners—Dialog Telekom, Infoshare, and USAID—met monthly in person or on a conference call, while a larger group of organizations, including QUALCOMM, Microsoft, and Lanka Orix, participated in conference calls on an as-needed basis.

Because every partnership is unique, it is important to tailor your governance system to serve your ultimate goal while meeting the needs of your partners and the expectations of your other stakeholders.

Partnership Management

Partners also need to decide how the partnership will be managed day to day. Who will provide project management support to ensure that activities happen as planned and on schedule? Who will organize governance meetings? Who will prepare reports, press releases, and other essential documents? These and other fundamental questions demand answers before the partnership swings into action.

Below are three commonly used structures to manage partnerships. They're presented in in order of complexity and cost from lowest to highest.

- o *In-house management.* For many partnerships, the easiest, most cost-efficient approach is for one of the partners to dedicate staff resources to providing the project management, facilitation, logistics, and reporting required. For example, in the partnership between Save the Children and Pearson, Save the Children serves in the role of partnership manager. The downside to this approach is that the management may be seen as favoring the interests of the host partner organization; it's important that the people given this responsibility avoid creating this impression.
- o *Third-party management.* For larger, more complex partnerships, a dedicated third-party manager may be

needed. This could be an individual, a consulting firm, or an NGO. One advantage to third-party management is that the manager can provide a high level of neutrality and objectivity. In addition, a consulting firm or an NGO can provide significant logistical and organizational support for travel, meetings, and events, as well as ensuring compliance and transparency. The downside, of course, is that hiring a third-party manager can add considerable costs to the partnership.

o *Partnership backbone organization or coordinator.* In some types of partnerships, particularly collective-impact partnerships, it may not be practical for one entity to act as the conduit for all activities across multiple organizations and geographies. In such cases, it may be more effective to establish a partnership coordinator whose main job is to bring partners together and ensure a shared, steady flow of information about activities.

o *Dedicated secretariat.* Large multi-stakeholder initiatives and other complex partnerships often require a dedicated secretariat to manage the day-to-day activities of the partnership. For example, the Global Alliance on Vaccines and Immunizations (GAVI) is a large, multibillion-dollar, multi-stakeholder initiative that maintains a secretariat with offices in Geneva, Switzerland, and Washington, D.C.

In Sri Lanka, we decided very quickly to manage the partnership in-house, with our team serving as the partnership manager. Why? First, this partnership was relatively small, which meant we had neither the resources nor the need to bring in a third-party manager. Second, over the process of developing and negotiating the partnership, the major partners—USAID, Dialog, and InfoShare—had built a high degree of mutual trust and alignment on vision. Therefore, we were ready to move forward together and did not need an additional cook in the kitchen.

Writing a Partnership Agreement

Once all the preceding steps have been completed, it's time to make things official with the writing of a partnership agreement. Partnership agreements can come in many forms and bear various names: a memoradum of understanding, a memorandum of agreement, a letter of intent, and so on. You'll want to have your in-house counsel or an outside attorney work on crafting this important document. What follows should not be considered legal advice, but rather a simple list of some of the elements your partnership agreement needs to cover.

- o *Description of partner organizations and their representatives.* Who are the partner organizations? Who is empowered to act upon the behalf of the partners?
- o *Goal or purpose.* What are the partners aiming to achieve through the partnership? What are the shared goals and objectives?
- o *Roles and responsibilities.* What roles will the various partners undertake in the partnership? What responsibilities will each partner have?
- o *Resource contributions.* What resources are the partners contributing to the partnership? Is there a specific

dollar amount of funding to be provided? Can other resources be quantified? What is the timetable by which the resources will be delivered?

o *Activities.* What activities or tasks will be completed under the partnership? Are there phases to the project or program? How will these be sequenced?

o *Governance and decision-making.* What governance structure will be established for the partnership?

o *Reporting.* How will information about activities and financials be shared among the partners and other stakeholders?

o *Ownership of revenues and intellectual property.* If the partnership is going to produce revenue flows or generate intellectual property, who will own or control these?

o *Publicity and branding.* What are the rules for publicizing the partnership through press releases, advertisements, social media, and other venues? What rules will govern the use of partner logos?

o *Confidentiality.* What information must be kept confidential?

o *Termination.* What is the process and timeline for withdrawing from the partnership?

o *Signators.* Who will sign the partnership agreement on behalf of the partner organizations?

If your partnership has more than two partners, a key decision you will need to make is whether to negotiate a single partnership agreement signed by all the partners or a series of bilateral agreements that you sign with each of the partners. In general, though a single agreement may take longer to negotiate, it is generally more transparent, since all parties agree to all aspects of the partnership, and therefore preferable.

Note that, in addition to the partners themselves, it may be useful to have critical external stakeholders sign on to the partnership agreement, perhaps as witnesses. For example, if a partnership is going to work in a particular locality, having a local government leader as a signator can help ensure buy-in at the community level.

When crafting a partnership agreement, the best practice is to refrain from making partner commitments legally binding. This simplifies some of the lawyering and puts the minds of corporate risk managers at ease. Partnerships are built on trust, and the agreement merely codifies that trust. By contrast, making a cross-sector partnership legally binding can create complications without providing significant benefits. If a partner fails to deliver on a commitment, how likely is it that your company would pursue a legal remedy?

If you need to invoke the law to get a partner to fulfill their commitments, your partnership is almost certainly dead already.

Crossing the Valley of Partnership Death

Crossing the Valley of Partnership Death is never easy. It requires patience, perseverance, flexibility, and empathy to take a promising idea and work through the many steps required to transform it into a signed and sealed partnership agreement.

For Pearson and Save the Children, the process of getting to a signed agreement took more than a year. Under the terms that the two organizations finally hammered out, the Every Child Learning Partnership leveraged the unique capabilities of both partners to provide vulnerable refugee children in Jordan with access to quality education services.

In Sri Lanka, we signed a series of memoranda of understanding with individual partners—Dialog Telekom, Qualcomm, Lanka Orix, InfoShare, and Microsoft—over the course of spring, 2007, in anticipation of a May launch.

And in Kenya, it took Medtronic a year to negotiate a memorandum of understanding with three county governments ("counties" being the Kenyan equivalent of states or provinces), the Kenyan Ministry of Health, Novartis Social Business, and an NGO named Management Sciences for Health.

Yet although arriving at a signed partnership agreement requires an arduous journey, it is, in Winston Churchill's memorable phrase, merely "the end of the beginning." In the next two chapters, we will focus on the steps that follow: implementing a partnership successfully and ensuring that it delivers results—for your business, for your cross-sector partners, and for your other stakeholders.

8

Implementation:
How to Get Things Done
Through Partnerships

- The six attributes of successful cross-sector partnership implementation, and how to achieve them
- How well-implemented partnerships can produce extraordinary results

Dateline: Bohol, Philippines. The setting for the partnership launch ceremony was picturesque: a chic eco resort overlooking the glimmering, crystal-blue waters of the Philippine Sea. Press photographers snapped photos as senior representatives from Microsoft, USAID, the Philippines Department of Science and Technology, and the country's Bureau for Aquatic Resources and Fisheries signed the partnership agreement to deploy the cutting edge technology of TV white space to connect remote fishing communities in the Philippines.

Sitting in the audience that day in spring, 2013, Microsoft's Damian "Dondi" Mapa watched the signing ceremony with a mixture of pride and trepidation. As Microsoft's national technology officer for the Philippines at the time, Dondi had played a key role in the design of the TV White Space partnership. The partnership was important to Microsoft because the legendary company was in the midst of the largest transformation in its history. As Dondi explains, "Microsoft was transitioning from selling software in boxes to selling cloud subscriptions over the Internet. For the cloud model to work, you need to have connectivity within the environment you are operating in." TV white space technology would provide that connectivity for the Philippines.

Sometimes called *dynamic spectrum allocation,* TV white space technology uses traditional television frequencies to deliver low-cost Internet coverage over vast distances, making it an attractive new option for previously unconnected populations. Microsoft was pioneering the technology in the hope of attracting new users to the company's cloud services.

But the TV white space technology was still unproven in real-world conditions. This was the genesis of the partnership. "We decided to do a pilot," Dondi explains. "We wanted to test it in an area where there was no Internet. We shortlisted several areas that looked like good use cases—education, health, governance. It just so happened that USAID had a use case for government fisher registration in areas without telecommunications." The hope was that the connectivity provided by the partnership would enable better coastal fisheries management in outlying areas of the Philippines.

However, as the partnership was launched, Dondi was nervous. Technology risk, relationship risk, execution risk—there was certainly a lot that could go wrong with this partnership. "There was a lot we did not know. We did not know how the technology would work in the real world. We did not know how well the partners would work together. What we did know was that there was tremendous potential," notes Dondi.

The moment when a partnership is launched is a time of great excitement—but also a time of uncertainty. PACE's David McGinty compares it to childbirth: "You can go to all the birth classes, but that doesn't prepare you for the minute after childbirth. In partnerships, you can do a lot of work getting to yes, but once that baby arrives, you have to use new tools and skills to raise it."

Sometimes the challenge of implementing a cross-sector partnership is complicated by inadequate prelaunch planning. Too often, the partners focus more on the public relations elements of the partnership than on its execution, basking in the glow of the announcement rather than getting down to brass tacks. The resulting problems can kill a promising partnership.

And just as when parents are raising a new child, the unexpected often happens. At the very time when the TV White Space Partnership was getting off the ground, the Philippines was struck by two catastrophic natural disasters. In October, 2013, the Bohol earthquake hit, killing more than 200. Less than a month later, Super Typhoon Yolanda (known elsewhere as Typhoon Haiyan) killed more than 6,000 people and left tens of thousands homeless. These tragic disasters that befell the Philippines in 2013 made the TV White Space Partnership exceptionally challenging to implement.

Fortunately, most cross-sector partnerships do not face such catastrophes. Nonetheless, like raising a baby, implementing partnerships can be exceptionally challenging, even under the best of circumstances. In this chapter, we'll explore the six attributes of successful partnership implementation.

- o Trust
- o Quick wins
- o Flexible, adaptive leadership
- o A high degree of accountability
- o Robust project management
- o Strong relationship management and communication

Trust

Trust might seem to be an obvious characteristic of any successful relationship, but it's worth calling out because it is so foundational for successful implementation of a cross-sector partnership. Trust is the glue that enables organizations with radically different mandates and organizational cultures to work toward a shared goal. When trust is lacking, it becomes almost impossible for partners to share information and feedback effectively, to resolve differences, and to deal unforeseen circumstances.

Here are some ways partners can foster trust.

Abide by first principles. In the previous chapter, we talked about the importance of establishing first principles that all the partners will adhere to. After the partnership is launched, partners need to revisit those first principles and renew their commitment to abiding by them during implementation.

Be open about your goals and intentions. We previously quoted PACE's David McGinty about the importance of having honest conversations with partners about your motivations. Sometimes the motivations you need to disclose may be personal ones—for example, you may hope that the partnership will help you earn a promotion to a coveted job. Letting your partners know about this will prevent them from being blindsided and perhaps feeling abandoned if and when the promotion comes through. In other cases, the motivations may be organizational ones—for instance, your NGO partner may hope to use the partnership as a springboard for fundraising in support of other, separate programs. By being clear about their intentions, partners minimize the possibility of misunderstanding and conflict.

Accept the legitimacy of partner goals and intentions. Be ready to accept the legitimacy of your partner's motivations, even if you do not fully share them. Accepting is not agreeing! A good corporate partner can accept the fact that a government partner may need to achieve a certain policy objective, even if that policy objective is not a goal shared by the company. Conversely, a good NGO partner can accept the legitimacy of a business partner's goals. For example, as PepsiCo's Rob Meyers points out, "It is important to find a good partner on the other side who doesn't cringe at the fact that you have to make a profit."

During implementation, be open and frank about your reactions to events. Corporate, government, and nonprofit partners will always perceive the world differently. In strong partnerships, the partners are open and honest about sharing their reactions to events and situations, especially those that are unexpected and demand a response from the partnership.

Be open to feedback, both positive and negative. Good partners are strong and self-confident enough to deal with honest feedback from their counterparts. When partners have opposing views about dealing with challenges, adjusting policies to changing circumstances, or taking advantage of opportunities, don't assume that the partnership is in danger. Seek to learn from the perspectives of your partners, and work to find common ground on which you can build a new consensus for the partnership's next phase.

Quick Wins

Successfully designing, building, and launching a partnership takes a big investment of time and energy, which often raises the internal stakes among the partner organizations. Avoid the common scenario in which a partnership is launched with great fanfare, then "goes dark" for months or years as the partners figure out how to work together and get things done.

When this happens, skeptics and even some supporters will begin to question the value of the partnership.

To prevent this, the partners should work together to create some quick wins that will demonstrate progress towards results. These do not need to be huge, but they need to be sufficiently visible to mollify the critics and skeptics. Look for achievements that:

- o Can be implemented within 90 days, thereby coinciding with the quarterly reporting cycles used by many companies and organizations
- o Have a low risk of failure and a high probability of success
- o Are relatively narrow and focused in scope, making them simple to explain and implement
- o Will promote buy-in by giving stakeholders something concrete to celebrate

In the case of the Every Child Learning partnership created by Pearson and Save the Children, Amanda Gardiner arranged to have the Pearson CEO announce a corporate grant to Save the Children UK. The funds would be used to implement key elements of their joint project to help children displaced by the Syrian conflict. The grant was a relatively small element of the partnership, but the formal announcement provided a sense of momentum in the early stages of the project. This bought the partners additional time to sort out the complexities of implementing a cross-sector partnership in the midst of one of the greatest refugee crises of the last half century.

Flexible, Adaptive Leadership

Not every partnership encounters an earthquake and a typhoon during implementation, as the Philippines TV White Space Partnership did. But almost every partnership faces significant challenges. Partners are often trying out a new, untested solution to a problem. Sometimes that solution may work; other times, it may be necessary for the partnership to pivot. Being an adaptive partnership leader requires the ability to be flexible in response to changing circumstances. It also requires the ability to link the partnership goals to the core values, abilities, and dreams of key stakeholders; the ability to create an environment where a diversity of viewpoints can be embraced and where the collective knowledge of the partners is leveraged to overcome challenges; the ability to be proactive and resourceful, constantly scanning for new opportunities and resources; and the ability to admit mistakes and learn from them.

If you can adapt and evolve your partnership in the light of changing circumstances, you can achieve success even when your plans go awry. As Microsoft's Dondi Mapa says, "Sometimes the goals we set are not the goals we meet, but the alternative goals we achieve are just as good or better."

A High Degree of Accountability

Another key factor that separates partnerships that succeed from those that founder is a high degree of accountability among the partners. In cross-sector partnerships, there are three dimensions to accountability.

○ *Accountability to partners.* First and foremost, partners need to be accountable to one another. This means fulfilling the specified roles and responsibilities and providing the agreed-upon resources. It also means communicating clearly and effectively, letting partners know if commitments are falling behind schedule or below expected levels, and sharing accurate information about how the partnership is meeting its goals—or failing to meet them.

○ *Accountability to external stakeholders.* It is critical that the partners hold themselves accountable, collectively and individually, to external stakeholders who may be interested in or impacted by the partnership: customers, intended beneficiaries, government bodies, watchdog groups, community organizations, and so. This requires regular communication, periodic partnership updates and, when appropriate, stakeholder consultations. Listen with an open mind to feedback from stakeholders, take their concerns seriously, and be ready to learn from their ideas.

○ *Accountability to internal stakeholders.* As we discussed in chapter six, stakeholders inside your company or organization are critical to your partnership's success. Therefore, it is important that you regularly share successes, failures, and lessons learned with those internal stakeholders.

Because cross-sector partnerships take on some of society's most challenging and complex problems, there are sure to be conflicts along the way. Disagreements, even serious ones, need not be fatal to a partnership, so long as they are handled with openness and honesty. If you behave in a way that shows you take the notion of accountability to heart, you'll likely find that your partners and stakeholders will give you the benefit of the doubt and remain supportive even when the partnership road gets rocky.

Robust Project Management

At the end of the day, partnerships are about G.T.D.—*getting things done.* In a complex context like cross-sector partnership, that requires robust project management to ensure that partner tasks are completed, resources supplied, and deadlines met.

Fortunately, project management is a core competency of many organizations—companies and NGOs alike—for which there are hundreds of tools and resources available. Here are a few you may want to employ when working on project management for your cross-sector partnership.

- o *The partnership scorecard.* This is a chart or table that breaks down partnership goals and activities into discrete tasks, assigns them to partners, sets deadlines, and tracks task completion. The partnership scorecard can be an excellent tool when partner activities involve distinct work streams that require coordination. One simple form of scorecard is a Google doc or Excel spreadsheet that partners can use to update their progress and review the work of the other partners. (A sample partnership scorecard appears in this book as Appendix B. You can find an interactive template to design your own partnership scorecard on the website for readers of this book at www.SteveSchmida.com.)

o *The stage-gating system.* If your partnership is developing a new and innovative solution to a problem—for example, a dedicated app, website, or software tool—a stage-gating system may be an effective project management tool. It breaks down the innovation process into distinct stages separated by decision points (stage gates), at which the partners review progress to determine whether they are ready to advance to the next stage. Figure 8-1 shows the structure of a sample stage-gating system that can be adapted for your own partnership project.

o *Documenting and Reporting.* As with any good project, there needs to be an appropriate level of documenting of decisions and actions taken, especially with regard to decision-making. Meeting notes, short activity summaries, and correspondence files can help ensure that there is a record of decisions and actions that can be referred back to when needed. Many partners choose to create a common online workspace, using collaboration tools such as Sharepoint, Slack, or Google Suite, where these documents can live. In the event of changes in staffing among partners, having a common archive of documents can help those new to the partnership get up to speed quickly.

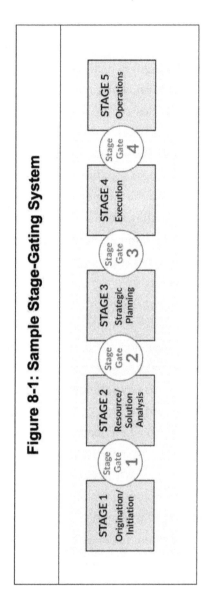

Figure 8-1: Sample Stage-Gating System

In the Philippines, the partners involved in the TV White Space Partnership employed the stage-gate system. At each stage gate, partners would meet together, review progress to date, and decide whether it was time to move on to the next stage of activity. The stage-gating process allows partners to move forward together while creating specific moments in time where they can assess progress, discuss differences, and align on a pathway forward.

Strong Relationship Management and Communication

Because partnerships are ultimately about relationships, strong relationship management and communication are vital to successful partnership implementation.

Here are some important characteristics of effective relationship management.

- ○ *Transparency.* Keep partners apprised of changes in your organization that impact the partnership. Rob Meyers recalls how a partnership was badly shaken when PepsiCo's business priorities changed dynamically. "Sometimes a business makes big decisions really quickly," he observes. When this happens—for example, if a new CEO decides to institute a change in corporate strategy that may force changes in the partnership's goals--your partners should find out about it from you personally, and preferably in advance, rather than reading about it after the fact on Bloomberg.

o   *Consultation.* Partners need to consult with one an-
     other before making fundamental changes to partner-
     ship-related activities, even those that might seem to
     fall completely within their own domain. When you
     belong to a partnership, you don't have the option of
     "going rogue," then expecting your partners to simply
     accept your decision or behavior.

o   *Consistency.* Partners need to establish a schedule of
     meetings or conference calls to review partnership
     progress—and then stick to that schedule. Between
     meetings, consider using multiple channels, such as
     instant messaging or collaboration tools like Slack and
     MS Teams, to ensure that information of immediate
     importance is being communicated quickly and
     clearly.

o   *Collegiality.* In addition to regular check-in meetings,
     create opportunities to build and deepen mutual un-
     derstanding and trust. Lunches, dinners, retreats, and
     other informal gatherings can play a vital role in
     strengthening the bonds that keep a partnership
     strong.

o   *External communication.* To outsiders, particularly in
     developing countries, a cross-sector partnership can
     appear strange, even menacing. A Fortune 500 com-
     pany, a leading NGO, and a government agency work-
     ing together can arouse suspicion that they have
     formed a cabal or conspiracy to exploit the poor. So it's
     essential to have a clear plan to communicate with ex-
     ternal stakeholders, including the press, civil society
     organizations, and community-level beneficiaries.

> When you're working on a particularly sensitive problem, consider taking extra steps to ensure transparency. In addition to one-way communication through press releases and websites, try two-way channels such as community consultations and advisory boards that allow stakeholders to better understand the goals and activities of the partnership. As U.S. President Lyndon Johnson supposedly said about FBI Director J. Edgar Hoover, "Better to have him inside the tent pissing out, than outside the tent pissing in."

In 2011, the giant American agricultural firm Monsanto partnered with USAID on a project intended to increase farmer incomes in a Nepal. Because the partners failed to communicate the purposes and activities of the partnership effectively to outside stakeholders, the local press stirred up accusations of modern-day imperialism, international NGOs launched angry accusations at company shareholder meetings, and in-country activists protested outside the U.S. embassy. Within months, the partnership fell apart.

The Rewards of Adroit Implementation

Implementing a partnership is never easy, but when the partnership is well-designed and effectively implemented, the results can be extraordinary. In the Philippines, the TV White Space Partnership proved to be a case in which flexibility and adaptability turned a near-debacle into a success.

The natural disasters that hit the Philippines shortly after the launch of the partnerships wiped out landline and cellular communications system in many outlying island communities.

But Microsoft, USAID, and their government partners were able to get the TV white space network up and running again within 48 hours of the Bohol earthquake. The connectivity the partnership provided made possible tens of thousands of Skype calls between first responders and government officials in Manila. These calls helped facilitate the rapid provision of aid to the communities, enabling them to move from crisis to recovery as regular telecommunications were restored.

The TV White Space Partnership ultimately achieved goals and expectations that exceeded the initial expectations of the partners. Microsoft got a high-profile demonstration that TV white space technology was a cost-effective and resilient method for connecting remote communities to the Internet. It also set the stage for increasing investment in telecommunications infrastructure across the country. And for USAID and the government of the Philippines, the partnership enabled outlying communities to use the TV white space technology to reach loved ones and access government services.

In 2015, Secretary of State John Kerry awarded the TV White Space Partnership the P3 Impact Award. The term "P3" refers to public-private partnerships that address societal problems, and the P3 Impact Award is an annual prize created by Concordia, the University of Virginia Darden School Institute for Business in Society, and the U.S. Department of State's Office of Global Partnerships, and presented each fall at the Concordia Summit in New York.

The award was a powerful validation of the social benefit created by the Philippines TV White Space Partnership. Following its success in the Philippines, Microsoft launched the Airband Initiative with the goal of bringing affordable broadband connectivity to millions of individuals and families in under-served regions of the rural United States and around the world. It seems that Microsoft has developed a deep appreciation for the business benefits that cross-sector partnerships can produce.

9

Measurement Matters

o   How to track and measure the results produced by a cross-sector partnership
o   Understanding and monitoring partnership fitness

Dateline: Kyrgyzstan. In the mid-1990s, I was living in one of the newest countries in the world. Nestled among the stunning mountains of Central Asia, Kyrgyzstan had gained its independence in 1991 when the Soviet Union collapsed.

During that time, I heard a story about a World Bank consultant who had been sent to a factory on the shores of Kyrgyzstan's Lake Issyk Kul to help the factory become more efficient and profitable. During Soviet times, the factory had manufactured and tested torpedoes for the Soviet Navy. After the collapse of the Soviet Union, torpedoes were no longer in demand in landlocked Kyrgyzstan. So the consultant was surprised to discover that the plant was still churning out torpedoes, piling stacks of them on the ground outside the factory. The consultant asked a factory manager about it.

"We are measured against the plan that the national authorities send us," the manager explained. "The plan has not changed, so our work remains the same."

The story may be apocryphal, but it illustrates the familiar management rule, "What gets measured, gets done."

It's important for a cross-sector partnership to demonstrate value to all its stakeholders, including its partners from business, civil society, and government as well as the communities, groups, and people who should benefit from its problem-solving efforts. This means the need to ensure that they are monitoring progress and measuring results in ways that are meaningful to their stakeholders—not just "manufacturing torpedoes" in accordance with an outdated and irrelevant plan.

In business, the field of performance measurement is vast, and companies invest significant sums to ensure that they are accurately tracking and monitoring the performance of their business units. How many widgets did our factories churn out this quarter? What is our staff turnover rate? How many impressions did we get on our website? How have our revenues, our profits, and our gross margin changed over the past year?

In the social development sphere, measuring results is equally important, and it can be even more complicated, in part because cause and effect may be difficult to prove. Did our job training program cause trainees to get jobs, or did unemployment decline because of general economic growth? Did maternal mortality fall because of the new perinatal program we established, or did rising community incomes lead to an improvement in nutrition and other health-related changes?

In cross-sector partnerships, we need to make sure that we are measuring results that matter. We also need to monitor the fitness of the partnership to ensure that it is meeting the needs of the partners as well as delivering results. In this chapter, we'll look at two tools that partners can use to monitor and measure the performance of their partnership: the *partnership results chain* and *the partnership fitness framework*.

The Partnership Results Chain

Partnerships are about getting things done; a partnership is just a means for doing it. To understand whether we are getting things done, we have to understand the chain of events that connects our motivations and goals to outputs and results. The partnership results chain is a tool for helping us follow that sequence. It consists of six links.

1. Partner motivations
2. The partnership goal
3. Partner inputs
4. Partner activities
5. Partnership outputs
6. Partnership results

The partnership results chain is designed to help partners from across business, government, and civil society understand what the partnership is achieving and what value it is creating for stakeholders. You'll want to begin drafting a partnership results chain early in the history of your partnership, so you can use it to monitor and measure the effectiveness of your activities as soon as they begin.

If you are partnering with a donor agency or an NGO, your partner may be familiar with the partnership results chain. It is based on *logical framework analysis* (often called simply *logframe*), a technique pioneered by the World Bank and widely used in the development and nonprofit communities.

The partnership results chain differs from logframe in two ways. First, it tries to capture and understand individual partner motivations, thereby ensuring that the interests of all the partners are adequately reflected and addressed.

Second, it leaves out *impact*, which is the final link in the cause-and-effect chain that logframe analyses. This might seem to be a surprising omission. After all, the purpose of most cross-sector partnerships is to achieve impact—so why leave it out?

The reason is important and takes a bit of explanation. In the social and development space, the term *impact* has a very specific meaning. It refers to the changes that can be attributed to a particular program, either intended and unintended. But defining impact in social and development programs is not easy, because partnerships do not operate in a sterile laboratory but in a messy and complicated world. In fact, it is so hard to measure impact in the real world that three development economists won the Nobel Prize for Economics in 2019 for devising a method of measuring impact by using randomized control trials similar to those used in the pharmaceutical industry during the drug approval process.

However, measuring impact through randomized control trials is time-consuming and very expensive; it can take years and cost millions of dollars. What's more, in many partnerships, having a control group and a treatment group is impractical.

Furthermore, while the findings from impact studies can be extremely important to policy experts and academics, they are less helpful to practitioners because they do not measure impact in real time but only years after a program is completed. What's more, the results achieved are often inconclusive and difficult for nonspecialists to parse and interpret.

For all these reasons, the partnership results chain does not include impact measurement. Instead, it focuses on measuring results in real time: How well is the partnership performing? Is it achieving its intended objectives?

Now let's dive into each link of the chain.

Partner Motivations

For a cross-sector partnership to be successful, each partner needs to get some value out of it—after all, that is why the partners are willing to invest time and money in the first place. The first link in the partnership results chain defines the motivation of each partner—the reason why the partner has signed on to the partnership.

For example, in the case of the Easy Seva partnership in Sri Lanka, here are some illustrative partner motivations:

- USAID: To increase the number of people in rural Sri Lanka who have access to information and services via broadband
- Dialog Telekom: To increase engagement with rural customers using affordable Dialog-enabled services
- QUALCOMM: To demonstrate the value of Qualcomm technology in delivering affordable broadband in rural areas
- Lanka Orix: To explore whether leasing PCs in rural communities could be a viable line of business
- Info-Share: To improve the ability of rural citizens to access and share information on human rights
- EasySeva owners and entrepreneurs: To develop profitable businesses delivering access to affordable broadband through small-scale Internet cafés
- Microsoft: To demonstrate how Microsoft office products can enhance lives of individuals living at the base of the economic pyramid

By clearly and succinctly defining partner motivations, you will be in a better position to ensure that the indicators you subsequently track correspond to partner motivations.

The Partnership Goal

The partnership goal is a clear and succinct summary of what the partners hope to achieve through collaboration.

In the case of the Sri Lanka Easy Seva partnership, the partnership goal was quite simple: "We will demonstrate that it is possible to provide access to affordable broadband Internet in rural communities in Sri Lanka on a sustainable basis."

Partner Inputs

Each partner contributes something of value to the partnership. These contributions, also known as *inputs*, can take many forms—funding, investment, expertise, technology, market access, legitimacy, network—depending on the focus, complexity, and goal of the partnership as well as the capabilities and resources of the partners. In the case of Sri Lanka, here are some examples of inputs:

- o From USAID: $380,000 in funding for staff and project management costs
- o From the U.S. ambassador and the USAID mission director: the ability to convene potential partners and stakeholders
- o From QUALCOMM: $250,000 in funding

- ○ From Dialog Telekom: access to 3G networking infra-structure and use of billing and customer service systems
- ○ From Lanka Orix: a lease package for PCs
- ○ From Microsoft: 240 Windows and Office Software licenses, and training in the use of PCs and software applications

Monitoring inputs is important for a couple of reasons. First, having a clearly defined list of inputs early in the partnership process can help everyone do a gut check as to whether the inputs planned are likely sufficient to deliver the desired result. Second, sharing the list of inputs helps partners hold one another accountable for delivering on their commitments.

Partner Activities

The partners use the inputs received to conduct activities aimed at achieving the intended goal. In the Sri Lanka case, for example, the partners conducted a wide range of activities in areas that included network and infrastructure building, entrepreneur selection and training, product design, marketing, customer support and billing, technical support, and more. The partnership scorecard, which we introduced in chapter eight, can be a useful tool for capturing and monitoring the implementation of partner activities.

Partnership Outputs

The term *outputs* refers to concrete, measurable products generated through the partner activities. For each activity, there should be one or more corresponding outputs that are tracked and measured, all under the direct control of the partners conducting the activity. For example, if a partnership conducts three training workshops, the number of people trained at those workshops would be the output. If a partnership is conducting market research, the market research report would be the output.

Partnership Results

The last link is results, where, hopefully, the payoff of the partnership can be monitored and measured. (In the World Bank's logframe system, results are referred to as *outcomes*, which is the term many NGOs and donors use. However, because most business professionals think in terms of results, we've decided to stick with that term here.)

Derived from the activities, results need to be clearly articulated and tracked through concrete indicators. We recommend using the acronym SMART to define your results indicators according to five criteria.

- o *Specific.* Be as clear as possible about what you want to achieve, defining it in terms that everyone can agree upon.
- o *Measurable.* Use indicators that can be tracked and measured in numerical terms. Cost may play a role in the indicators you develop, since some indicators are

relatively easy to track and measure, while others can be very expensive. But within the limits of practicality, the more precisely measurable, the better.

- *Achievable.* For the partnership to have a reasonable chance of success, each indicator needs to be achievable within a realistic time frame and at an affordable cost.
- *Relevant.* The achievement of each indicator should contribute demonstrably to the partnership goal.
- *Timely.* Indicators need to be time-bound, with subsidiary benchmarks to help track progress toward their achievement.

Let's see how we applied the SMART approach to creating indicators for use in tracking the results of the Sri Lanka partnership. As you recall, the partnership goal was, "We will demonstrate that it is possible to provide access to affordable broadband Internet in rural communities in Sri Lanka on a sustainable basis." Let's break that statement down into its essential components and see how they contributed to the indicators we selected.

"To provide access." This means that people in rural Sri Lanka had to have the ability to get online in a way that was relatively straightforward and accessible. Given that we were using an Internet café model, we decided to track this result using the following measurable indicators:

- Number of towns with populations from of 2,000 to 10,000 people with an Easy Seva café
- Number of people living in communities with an Easy Seva café

o Number of Easy Seva customers per month

"Affordable broadband internet." Here, we focused on two sets of indicators:

o *Price.* At the time, Internet access was extremely expensive in rural Sri Lanka (if available at all), with prices running over $2/hour for 64 kilobits-per-second dial-up. The goal of the partnership was to bring that price down by at least an order of magnitude.

o *Internet speed.* At the time, broadband was still a relatively new concept that lackedan agreed-upon definition, particularly in developing countries. Together with our partners at QUALCOMM and Dialog, we looked at the capabilities of the 3G and WiMax technologies and determined that 712 kilobits per second would be a quantum leap over the existing 64 kilobits-per-second speed and achievable with the technology available at the time.

"On a sustainable basis." We did not have funding to subsidize the cost of the Internet cafés. Thus, if the effort was to be sustainable, the cafés had to operate as businesses, earning enough revenue to cover their costs (including equipment depreciation) over time. We did some financial modeling and came up with the following metrics:

o Percentage of Easy Seva Internet café owners grossing more than $200 per month

o Percentage of Easy Seva Internet cafés in operation at least six months after the launch of the partnership

As you can see, breaking down the partnership goal statement into its component parts enables you to develop categories of results indicators. A helpful resource you can turn to in this process is the United Nations' Sustainable Development Goals (described in chapter seven), which include more than 100 indicators, each linked to a specific goal. In addition, the Global Impact Investment Network (GIIN) has developed an extensive and detailed indicator library called IRIS+. IRIS+ indicators align with the SDGs as well as with protocols from the Global Reporting Initiative (GRI), the most widely accepted system for reporting on company sustainability efforts. Using the IRIS+ indicators makes good sense, especially if your company participates in the GRI program.

When choosing indicators, it is important to reexamine partner motivations to ensure that the things you're measuring are aligned with those motivations. Partners will often value indicators of success differently. Participating in the exercise of figuring out what will be monitored and measured can help partners develop a better understanding of their counterparts' motivations and needs.

If it's too difficult or expensive to directly measure a specific result a partner is looking for, you may need to develop a *proxy indicator*. This is an indirect measurement that can help partners infer whether a result is being achieved. For example, it was not cost-effective for us to measure how many Easy Seva customers were actually using the Microsoft Office applications on the PCs in the Internet cafés; the software needed to obtain such a measurement was too expensive and hard to use at the time. So the partners decided simply to count the number of customers using Easy Seva PCs—not an exact measure of MS Office use, but a reasonable proxy that was much easier and cheaper to monitor.

In addition to the cost of data collection, another consideration is timeliness. Some indicators can only be measured after the fact, meaning there is a significant lag before the data can be used for decision-making. In selecting indicators, consider whether you can get the data in time to use it in making decisions and adjusting your activities.

Now let's see how the indicators we developed for the Easy Seva partnership could be used to determine whether or not the partnership was successful.

Remember the partnership goal statement: "We will demonstrate that it is possible to provide access to affordable broadband Internet in rural communities in Sri Lanka on a sustainable basis." Let's map that goal statement against the actual results of the partnership:

- o *Access in rural communities:* The Easy Seva partnership made broadband access available to more than 100,000 Sri Lankans living in 55 small towns and villages across the island.
- o *Affordable:* The cost to the customers was an order of magnitude lower, and the connection speeds were five to ten times faster, than previously available alternatives.
- o *Sustainable:* More than 80 percent of the Internet cafés were operational and grossing in excess of $200 per month six months after the dissolution of the partnership.

Based on these indicators, we can see that the partnership definitely delivered against its goal.

Finally, remember that the results you are seeking to capture should be tied back to the first link in the chain: partner motivations. Figure 9-1 breaks down the Sri Lanka case by partner and ties results indicators to the motivations of the respective partners.

Figure 9-1: Sri Lanka Results as Sought by Partners

	Dialog	USAID and InfoShare	Qualcomm	Microsoft	Lanka Orix
Partner motivation	Increase rural customer awareness and lock-in	Improve rural Internet access	Demonstrate 3G technology	Increase access to MS Office applications	Pilot leasing of low-cost PCs in rural areas
Number of small towns		X			
Population of small towns		X			
EasySeva customers	X	X		X	

	Dialog	USAID and InfoShare	Qualcomm	Microsoft	Lanka Orix
Consumer broadband price	×		×		
Internet speed	×		×		
High-grossing EasySevas*	×				×
Surviving EasySevas+	×	×		×	×

* Percentage of EasySevas grossing over $200 per month.
+ Percentage of EasySevas open six months after launch of the partnership.

Notice that each partner had at least one or two results indicators that aligned with their motivations. The presence of this direct linkage between motivation and results helped ensure that we were tracking results important to each partner even as the partnership drove towards its higher-level goal.

Other Measurement Matters

You can achieve a deeper understanding of the results your partnership is achieving by measuring it against a *baseline assessment* of the problem you are trying to solve. A baseline assessment is conducted before the activities of the partnership get underway, providing the basis for a before-and-after comparison that can help you measure progress towards your goal. A good baseline assessment can also help you figure out the best indicators to measure.

There are a couple of downsides to doing a baseline assessment. One is time. A baseline assessment may take weeks or months to complete, depending on the level of complexity involved. Another is cost. Baseline assessments can get expensive quickly, often costing tens if not hundreds of thousands of dollars to complete. However, if you decide to forgo a baseline assessment, at least perform some research to gather basic data regarding the current situation before your partnership begins to work.

Another measurement point relates to the importance of *gender-disaggregated data.* At every stage of the monitoring process, beginning with the baseline assessment, make a point of collecting data in which results are differentiated by gender. The reason is that companies, NGOs, and government agencies today have become increasingly sensitive to the issue of gender equity. What's more, social scientists and researchers now recognize that gender differences and biases have a bigger impact on survey and study results than formerly recognized. Thus, it's important to ensure that any data you collect tracks numbers of men and women within their indicators. This will give you greater visibility on the extent to which the partnership is promoting gender equity.

Partnership Fitness

Everyone has heard the famous observation by Russian author Leo Tolstoy: "Happy families are all alike; every unhappy family is unhappy in its own way." Something similar applies to cross-sector partnerships. Happy partnerships have some basic qualities in common: strong alignment among partners, efficient management, mutual respect, and so on. Unhappy partnerships suffer breakdowns in one or more of these areas, leading to wasted time and resources, disgruntled stakeholders, and social problems that fester rather than being solved.

The *partnership fitness framework* (Figure 9-2) is a simple way to help partners monitor, measure, and understand the health of their partnership.

Figure 9-2: Partnership Fitness Framework

Operational Fitness	Relationship Fitness	Financial Fitness	Alignment
• *Efficiency:* How efficient is the partnership at making and executing decisions? • *Effectiveness:* How is the partnership performing in relation to its Results Chain?	• *Respect:* How well do partners understand and respect their counterparts' points of view? • *Mutuality:* How willing are partners to assist one another to overcome challenges and barriers? • *Engagement:* How well are partners participating at levels appropriate to their roles and responsibilities?	• *Resources:* Are partners contributing resources in accordance with commitments? • *Financial management:* How well is the partnership managing financial flows? • *Transparency:* Is there sufficient transparency among partners and stakeholders?	• *Partner alignment:* Are partners in agreement about partnership vision, goals, and objectives? • *Internal alignment:* Are partners fully supportive and engaged? • *Stakeholder alignment:* How well does the partnership garner and use feedback from external stakeholders?

Depending on the size and complexity of the partnership, partners can use the partnership fitness framework in different ways. In a joint project, the partners may simply want to talk through the different components of the framework periodically to make sure that the partnership is on track. In a more complex scenario, say a multi-stakeholder initiative, partners may conduct surveys among stakeholders or hold workshops to delve deeply into the various elements of partnership fitness.

Monitoring partnership fitness is a critical component in ensuring the success of a cross-sector partnership. Because companies, NGOs, and government agencies have such different organizational goals and cultures, it is easy for a partnership to get into trouble because of simple misunderstandings, inadequate communication, organizational breakdowns, and similar problems. The partnership fitness framework helps partners take stock and ensure that their collaboration is healthy and able to deliver value for the partners and stakeholders alike.

We did not have the partnership fitness framework when we were launching the Easy Seva Partnership in Sri Lanka, but I wish we had. While the partnership was successful, it had a number of challenges, particularly with respect to alignment of some of the partners, that we probably could have surfaced and dealt with more quickly and easily if we'd had access to the framework. Taking an intentional approach to measuring both the performance and the fitness of a partnership can help partners ensure that their collaboration stays on track and, hopefully, generates the desired results, both for the partners and for society as a whole.

10

Moving Up or Moving On

o   The three pathways to scaling a successful cross-sector partnership
o   The prerequisites for scaling products, services, and innovations created through a partnership
o   Sustaining the results of a partnership
o   Ending and exiting a partnership responsibly

Dateline: Jamestown, Ghana. The first thing you notice when you visit Jamestown is the energy. People are everywhere, all in motion. Traders with goods loaded on bikes and carts make their way through the crowded streets, bound for markets in central Accra. Women on the beach tend stoves in which the morning's catch is being smoked, fanning the coals with strips of cardboard. Men sit on the jetty mending their fishnets or fixing outboard motors. Children laugh and play among the wooden dugout fishing boats lined up along the shoreline. Jamestown may be poor, but it buzzes with energy and life.

With its high-powered vibe and disheveled, tumbledown colonial buildings, the Jamestown district of Accra exudes a certain easy charm. But the community's vibrancy hides a dark, tragic past. Until the 19th century, Jamestown was a port through which slaves were shipped to colonies in North and South America. After the slave trade ended, Jamestown became a fishing community and trading center. Early each morning, fishers board small, rickety dugout canoes and sail out to fishing grounds in the open ocean. Hours later, they bring the day's catch to shore for smoking, then sell it in street stalls and markets across Accra.

Life in Jamestown has never been easy. But, in recent years, things have gotten much harder. Population growth means that more fishers are on the water pursuing an ever-dwindling number of fish. The depleted fish stocks mean that fishers now have to travel more than a hundred miles across the open ocean to find fishing grounds. They often incur heavy debts to repair their boats or buy fuel. These challenges make fishing a risky livelihood for the fishers and their families alike. An accident at sea can leave a fisher out of work and a family destitute.

To the business executive from New York or London, Jamestown might seem an odd locale for taking to scale a new product in financial technology (or *fintech*). But the partners behind Fishers' Future Plan (FFP) saw past Jamestown's obvious challenges. Jamestown's fishers are a small part of Ghana's vast informal economy, an estimated 70 percent of the country's population of 24 million who are engaged in informal livelihoods such as fishing, farming, and small-scale trading—a market population larger than the entire population of the Netherlands or Belgium. That made Jamestown an exciting place to test a promising new financial tool.

A partnership among several Ghanaian insurance companies, Vodafone-Ghana, and USAID, FFP helps the fishers of Jamestown manage their high-risk work by letting them buy an innovative mobile microinsurance product directly over their mobile phones. A pilot project originally targeting 300 paying customers ending up attracting more than 3,000, a strong indication that FFP was offering something that customers valued.

Along the way, the leaders of FFP needed to manage the project with flexibility and opportunism. One reason was a surprising discovery they made about the market for their financial product. Rather than particularly valuing the insurance component of the service, the customers proved to be more interested in the ability to accumulate savings using their phones. Based on this early feedback, the partners quickly updated the FFP features to enhance the savings component.

A second surprise that demanded flexibility arose less than a year into the launch of FFP when a key partner, Bima Insurance, announced that it was leaving the partnership due to an internal organizational restructuring. "We were hit very hard by Bima's decision," Terry Amartei recalls. Terry is the coordinator for microinsurance at miLife, another of FFP's insurance company partners. Bima had provided FFP's sales and customer service platform, which meant that an abrupt departure could spell the end of the partnership.

The immediate challenge was an urgent need for communication with stakeholders. "Many of the communities where we were working had had bad experiences with financial service providers in the past," Terry says. "Some bad actors simply disappeared with customers' money." The FFP partners dreaded the idea that their customers would now associate their service with the same level of unreliability. Terry emphasizes, "We knew we had to be transparent with our customers. So we sent them messages explaining what was going on. We also reassured them that their savings balances were safe—which they were."

The second challenge was to manage the operational disruption caused by Bima's departure. Fortunately, the FFP partnership agreement had been carefully designed to mitigate the risk of losing a partner. It stipulated that Bima needed to provide a basic level of support for one year, which gave the remaining partners time to adapt. They were able to find a new service provider that could plug the hole left by Bima's departure with no interruption in service. "We even used the downtime to develop some new features for customers," Terry Amartei says. "We reduced prices and made it easier for customers to make savings deposits. Vodafone also added an autodebit feature, which is proving popular with customers."

What sustained the partnership during this tricky period? "Trust was key," Terry says. "We had the trust of the chiefs and other leaders in the local communities. We made sure we serviced these customers as best we could. As a result, we held our own until we were able to find a permanent solution to the problem." Not only did FFP survive the departure of Bima, but the partnership came out stronger for it.

Following the success of the pilot, the FFP corporate partners—miLife, Millennium Insurance, and Vodafone-Ghana—saw a strategic opportunity in serving large numbers of consumers in the informal economy. Terry is emphatic on this point: "Mobile money is the next big thing to hit Africa. Once you have mobile money, you can have access to insurance and other financial service products. We are talking about farmers, fishers, and other informal segments. We want to target rural folks and those involved in agrarian activities."

To capitalize on this opportunity, the partners would now need to think about how to scale up the FFP product from a few coastal communities in Ghana to reach consumers across the country.

If you follow the tech industry, you know that scaling has been a cornerstone of Silicon Valley dogma for a long time. Internet companies like Google and Facebook scaled with incredible speed because, once these companies had made a significant upfront investment in getting their technology to work, the incremental cost of adding new users on the Internet was effectively zero. What's more, these companies benefited enormously from *network effects*: The more users there are on a social media platform like Facebook, the more valuable the network, both to users and to paying customers such as advertisers. The magic of scaling is what transformed companies like these from dorm-room startups into giant corporations in just a few years.

PayPal and LinkedIn founder Reid Hoffman has described the magic of rapid growth using the term *blitzscaling*. "When you scale at speed," Hoffman says, "you can capture the market quickly and also outmaneuver potentially global competition. Given the parallels with military and sports strategies, we can call this blitzscaling. Literally: lightning scaling."

Blitzscaling sounds great, but it only works under a few key conditions.

- Your product or service is mobile or Internet-based and can be updated and improved continually without causing customer experience or safety problems
- Your product or service has low to zero incremental costs, meaning it costs virtually nothing to add new users or customers
- You have access to virtually unlimited capital and are not concerned about covering operating costs or profitability in the near term
- Your model is not constrained by physical world limitations: regulations, geography, infrastructure, and so on

If your partnership and the products, services, or goods it generates do not meet these requirements—and most do not—you cannot blitzscale in the manner of a Silicon Valley start-up. You need to think about scaling in a different way.

Getting Real About Getting to Scale

As applied to most innovative products and services, scaling is hard. The real world throws up all kinds of barriers and constraints that make scaling difficult and time-consuming. In fact, a 2014 analysis of cross-sector partnerships and other social innovations determined that it can often take a decade or more to scale.

When we think about scale in the context of cross-sector partnerships, we are usually not talking about scaling the partnership itself. We are referring to scaling up the *results* of the partnership, specifically the product or service innovations that are generating business value as well as positive social or environmental impacts. For example, the FFP partnership generated a new mobile-enabled microinsurance product for fishers in Ghana; the Every Child Learns Partnership created a new set of high-quality education services for Syrian refugees in Jordan. Scaling up these initiatives would mean finding ways to bring these products and services to a larger marketplace.

In addition, scaling can mean different things to different people and in different contexts. Harvard's Clayton Christensen talks about scaling in two dimensions: depth and breadth. Depth is going deep into a particular market segment—say, informal workers in Ghana. Breadth is offering a product or service across a range of market segments or geographies—say, informal workers in countries throughout sub-Saharan Africa.

In some industries, the above two points might seem obvious, but when working across sectors, they may not be readily understood. Therefore, when participants in a cross-sector partnership consider scaling, it is critically important for partners to

194

agree on what is to be scaled and what constitutes scale—breadth, depth, or both?

In addition, there are three prerequisites to scaling the product or service innovation of a cross-sector partnership.

- o *Benefits of scaling that increase more quickly than the costs of scaling.* Scaling only makes sense if the value derived from scaling increases faster than the costs. This value may be in the form of business value for a company, in the form of societal or environmental value for a government ministry or NGO, or, ideally, both.

- o *Proven willingness to pay for or invest in the product or service.* Scaling costs money. Therefore, there must be a stakeholder who is willing to pay for or invest in scaling up because it is demonstrably better than an existing alternative.

- o *An organizational structure with visionary leadership capable of managing scale-up.* Scaling is a difficult process that demands not only managerial and organizational capacity but also visionary leadership to execute successfully. Therefore, it requires an organization—a company, a government ministry, a network of NGOs, or some other group—that has the capacity to handle the process of scaling.

If your partnership meets these three criteria, you *may* have an opportunity to scale. You next need to consider carefully which pathway the partnership will take to scale. There are three main options: a private, market-based pathway; a public-sector-led pathway; and a private-public hybrid.

Scaling Pathway 1: A Private, Market-Based Pathway

The first and most powerful way to scale innovation is by unleashing market forces. If a partner or other stakeholder sees an opportunity to create business value by scaling up a solution, they can drive investment that can help fuel growth and expansion. For example, PepsiCo sees tremendous financial potential in a new women's economic empowerment partnership. If PepsiCo can demonstrate that empowering women in its agricultural supply chains will improve productivity and reliability of supply, the company will have a powerful driver for scaling across their global business, motivated by the most basic business force: the desire for increased profits.

There are three ways a market-based approach can scale innovation: through partner investment, through outside investment, and through organic growth. Let's take a quick look at each.

Partner investment. The most obvious approach is for one or more partners or other stakeholders in a partnership to make the investments needed to scale the innovation.

In Ghana, following the success of the FFP pilot, the corporate partners, including miLife, Millennium Insurance, and Vodafone-Ghana, got together and decided to capitalize on the market opportunity they saw in delivering a quality mobile microinsurance product to customers in Ghana's large informal economy. The first step was to make some improvements to the product so that it would appeal to a wide range of consumers in the informal economy. These included new features that would allow users to make deposits using the mobile app at any time and in unlimited amounts. Vodafone also introduced an auto debit feature to make repeated transactions easy and convenient. The enhanced product was relaunched in early 2020, with the goal of reaching 200,000 paying customers.

As the partnership scales mobile microinsurance across Ghana, the partners find they are creating value beyond the business opportunity. According to Terry Amartei, "The social impact is a big thing for Vodafone, miLife, and Mill. We are driving financial inclusion, and we are helping people take charge of their futures with insurance." However, it is the business opportunity that primarily motivated the partners to invest their own money in taking this innovation to scale.

Outside investment. In 2005, I landed my first paid assignment as a partnership consultant for USAID's Global Development Alliance. I was sent to Vietnam to help broker an education partnership with Microsoft a first for USAID. At the time, shared value was not yet a defined concept, but it was clear that we needed to focus the partnership in a manner that delivered results for both Microsoft and USAID.

Microsoft, was eager to train Vietnamese youth with information and communications technology (ICT) skills in hopes of making them Microsoft customers. USAID was eager to help Vietnam update its antiquated education system. Through a series of facilitated meetings, the partners decided to focus on bolstering ICT workforce skills through Vietnam's vocational education system. We soon brought QUALCOMM and HP to the table as partners as well.

The partnership was quickly swelling in scope and ambition, but to deliver on-the-ground results, we needed to find an organization capable of managing the partnership—one with strong management skills as well as a knowledge of and connection with Vietnam's education system.

We met with most of the USAID implementer community—chiefly contractors and NGOs—and were unimpressed. At the time, these organizations were not interested in partnerships; they just wanted USAID to give them money to implement their own development projects.

Then we met Tuan Pham, holder of an MBA from New York University, who was the head of a business incubator called CRC-TOPICA at Hanoi University of Technology. Tuan impressed us from the start. His strong leadership skills had enabled him to bootstrap his incubator from nothing. He was exactly what we needed to drive this partnership forward.

The partners decided that CRC-TOPICA was the ideal organization to implement the partnership. The Topic64 Alliance was formally launched in 2006 at a gathering attended by Bill Gates, then the CEO of Microsoft, the U.S. ambassador to Vietnam, and a group of senior Vietnamese government officials. The partnership went on to enable more than 100,000 vocational students to receive internationally recognized certifications for IT skills—impressive results by any standard.

Then something interesting and unexpected happened. Tuan saw a business opportunity in providing e-learning services to Vietnam's burgeoning youth population. In response, he converted the Topic64 Alliance into a private company named Topica. This decision was controversial at the time. Some of the partners had deep reservations about it, wanting the partnership itself to carry the work forward. At the time, the partners had committed less than two million dollars to the Topic64 Alliance.

However, Tuan's business instincts proved to be correct. Over the next decade, Topica quickly grew into Vietnam's largest e-education provider. It now employs 1,400 people across the region and has trained more than a million people. What's more,

Topica has attracted considerable outside investment. The results of a recent Series D round of investments imply that Topica's value is now in excess of $100 million—an investment of more than 50× the contribution of the partners a decade earlier. If the partners had been venture investors, results like these would place Topica in the top tier of successful venture capital investments. And with the market continuing to grow at an exponential pace, the future prospects are bright. According to Tuan (speaking in 2016), "Within 10 years, 50 per cent of students will receive their education via online."

This was a case in which none of the original business partners saw the potential business value in scaling the innovation. That left an opportunity for a different stakeholder to step to the plate—which Tuan has done very successfully.

Here are three key factors that can help to make a partnership into an attractive candidate for scaling through outside investment.

- o *Strong alignment among partners.* The Topic64 alliance partners—Microsoft, USAID, QUALCOMM, and IIP—were all well aligned around the goal of upgrading the ICT skills of Vietnamese youth. This made the partnership successful and paved the way for its subsequent explosive growth as a for-profit enterprise.
- o *The right resources from partners.* The partners did not just invest financial resources; they also brought additional value to bear. For example, the fact that Microsoft's Bill Gates traveled to Vietnam to launch the partnership in 2006 raised the profile of the Topic64 Alliance tremendously.

o *Strong leadership team.* Most venture investors will tell you they invest in people, not companies, and the Topic64 alliance is a case in point. Tuan's visionary leadership was the most important factor in turning Topic64 from a successful partnership into a scaled social enterprise delivering both business value and social benefits across Southeast Asia.

The journey of Topica shows how a partnership can be a useful tool for business incubation, serving as a testing group for derisking an early-stage, impact-focused venture. It is also a powerful example of how cross-sector collaboration can empower a visionary entrepreneur to drive impact at scale.

Organic Growth. The final approach to market-based scaling is via organic growth—that is, fueling growth through increased revenue. This can be achieving by creating new products or services; allocating retained earnings to invest in the business; improving key business metrics (reducing costs, increasing customer retention, and so on), or by some combination of all three.

The advantage to scaling through organic growth is that it does not require additional investment. However, it can be a slow, arduous, and uncertain process.

Scaling Pathway 2: A Public Sector-Led Pathway

Using market forces to scale makes sense when a partnership generates a product, good, or service that can readily be monetized. However, some partnerships produce results that can't be monetized, although they benefit society as a whole and often generate business value as a secondary impact. For example, a workforce development program produces a public good that directly benefits employers by providing them with a skilled labor force. However, while the business value may be real and meaningful, few companies view themselves as having either the means or the mandate to invest in a public good like a workforce development program. In this case, the most likely pathway to scale is one led by a public-sector organization such as a government agency.

The Every Child Learning Partnership created by Pearson and Save the Children offers another example. In Jordan, as in many other countries (including the United States), primary education is viewed as a public good that is delivered principally by the government. Therefore, if the partnership's program to deliver high-quality education to Syrian refugees and host community children in Jordan was to grow to scale, it was clear that the government of Jordan would have a very important role to play.

Amanda explains how the process unfolded. "Initially, we had to trust Save the Children to navigate the relationship with the government of Jordan, which also had implications for our business relationship with the government. Therefore, we ended up rolling out the program first to out-of-school youth to build trust and a track record with the government." The program's results were sufficiently promising that the Jordanian government decided that joining the partnership was worthwhile.

In 2016, the government signed an agreement with the partners providing access to the government school system. The Every Child Learning Partnership now has the potential to scale if Jordan's ministry of education sees sufficient value in its educational program, technology, and curriculum. For Pearson, this is a major win, because, if the government of Jordan begins to invest in technology-based education solutions, it is more likely to buy Pearson products and services in the future. In essence, the partnership may help to create a future growth market for the company.

As this story illustrates, engaging host governments takes time and patience. *Expect to invest time in building trust.* Government agencies and their managers generally operate under intense scrutiny from political leaders, the news media, and the public. They are appropriately cautious about collaborating with private entities. Be prepared to devote time to earning their trust.

Here are some other important steps to take when considering scaling via the public sector.

- ○ *Align with government objectives.* The more closely the goals of the partnership are aligned with the priorities of government leaders, the more likely those leaders are to engage and feel a sense of ownership.

- ○ *Identify the levels of government you need to engage with—local, provincial, national, international.* It can take time to figure out which social functions are managed by specific levels of government. If you hope to achieve scale at an international or global level, you'll also need to consider whether multilateral institutions like the European Union, the African Union, or the Association of Southeast Asian Nations (ASEAN) may need to be involved.

- ○ *Create space for government to lead.* Government partners may bristle if not given the opportunity to demonstrate leadership. When government is a critical partner, NGO and business partners need to give space for the public sector to lead.

The public-sector scaling pathway sometimes gets dismissed by free-market ideologues, but it is often a vital channel for bringing public goods to scale. Most governments have the mandate, resources, and mechanisms to scale up products or services that deliver value for their citizens, so you should be open to working with them when appropriate.

Scaling Pathway 3: A Private-Public Hybrid

The private-public hybrid pathway leverages the strengths of both the market and the public sector. When well managed, this can be a powerful way to bring innovation to scale.

In Africa, Medtronic Labs' new model of care for hypertension, dubbed Empower Health, showed promise following a small-scale pilot program involving about 150 patients. Feeling encouraged, the company began to think about scaling. But as Medtronic Labs' Chemu Lang'at says, "For a novel model of care, the big question is, who is willing to pay?"

The answer was not immediately obvious. Every country has a different approach to health care service delivery. Insurance companies, health care providers, employers, government health ministries, patients themselves—all could be potential customers for the Empower Health program. In developing economies like Ghana and Kenya, health systems are still nascent, making answering the question of who pays even less obvious.

In order to explore the expansion of Empower Health, Chemu and the Medtronic Labs team knew that they needed a better understanding of the local health care market. To gain this knowledge, Medtronic Labs launched a new partnership in 2018 with an array of organizations that were deeply knowledgeable about the Kenyan health care system. Afya Dumu (Kiswahili for "prosperous, lasting health") includes three Kenyan county governments; the national ministry of health; Novartis Social Business, a division of the Swiss pharmaceutical company dedicated to improving health case access, particularly in regard to chronic disease treatment and management; and Management Sciences for Health, a U.S.-based NGO focused on global health care problems.

Thus, Afya Dumu is a private-public hybrid partnership whose ultimate goal will be to bring the innovation hypertension program created by Medtronic Labs to scale. The process is starting with a pilot project based in three counties of Kenya. At the time of writing (fall, 2019), Afya Dumu has about 5,000 patients under active management care and nearly two dozen paying customers, mostly employers, insurers, and health care providers. If this initial scale-up proves successful, the partnership will scale nationwide.

The private-public hybrid model for scaling can make sense under the following circumstances:

o   The product or service is one for which the government normally plays a large role as buyer or investor
o   The product or service needs to be derisked before the private sector can fully invest
o   The product or service advances government goals, but the government lacks the resources or mandate to fully bear the costs

Paths to Sustainability

Not every partnership needs to scale. If the problem you seek to solve is confined to a single geography, community, or institution, it may not be necessary or even desirable for the partnership to scale. However, you may want the solution your partnership has generated to continue in some form, even if the partnership itself dissolves. As we've seen, the ability of the positive results generated by a partnership to persist without ongoing support from the partners is what constitutes sustainability in the world of partnerships.

What follows are some key questions that you and your partners can explore in order to uncover paths to sustainability for your partnership or for its positive impact on the world.

Does the solution created by your partnership lead to a revenue or business opportunity for a partner or a stakeholder? If so, could it generate revenue sufficient to cover ongoing costs? A partnership that creates a revenue or business opportunity is the easiest kind to sustain, provided that opportunity can be captured by a partner or stakeholder.

In the case of the Easy Seva centers in Sri Lanka, there were two parties interested in the business opportunity the centers created. One was the entrepreneurs who owned and operated the centers. Research conducted by Microsoft found that more than 80 percent of the centers were operating profitably more than a year after the partnership had ended. The second interested party was the mobile operator Dialog Telekom, which saw the centers as a new and potentially interesting pathway for customer acquisition in rural areas. Once the partnership ended, the entrepreneurs and Dialog continued to develop and support the centers as sources of revenue and customer engagement.

Does a partner or stakeholder see sufficient value in the solution to justify paying for the on-going costs? In the case of the partnership between the Eurasia Foundation and Texaco, Caspian State University committed to covering the ongoing staffing and connectivity costs of the law library and the Internet center after funding from the partnership ended. In this case, a public institution—the university—had a strong incentive to maintain the program as a benefit for its students and professors. Of course, the partner or stakeholder must also have sufficient resources to support the solution for as long as that support is needed.

Does the solution require long-term changes to behavior or practices by individuals, markets, or organizations? If so, what kinds of incentives need to be created or reinforced to encourage stakeholders to continue the changed behavior? In the case of the TV White Space Partnership in the Philippines, the pilot deployment of Internet technology did not spur the immediate use of the technology itself, which was the changed behavior sought by the partners. However, the partnership showed the market that there was demand for Internet in remote communities, creating an opportunity both for the incumbent telecommunications firms and for possible new players in the market. This caused the incumbent firms to increase their investments in telecommunications infrastructure. It also spurred the entry of a new telecommunications operator that has invested heavily in building out connectivity in remote areas of the country.

According to Microsoft's Dondi Mapa, the creation of the partnership "started a virtuous cycle. The partnership created more bandwidth in remote areas, which pushed new players to provide connectivity that was affordable. Supply drove demand, and more supply drove more demand." The expanded network created new opportunities for Microsoft to sell its products. Meanwhile, the government of the Philippines achieved a major policy objective by increasing access to affordable telecommunications services in remote areas, thereby improving the quality of life of local residents.

In this case, sustainability required a fundamental shift in market dynamics—a shift that helped both the government and Microsoft achieve their long-term goals.

Sometimes a partnership seeks to change behaviors at the individual level. For example, the Global Handwashing Partnership is a multistakeholder initiative including donors, NGOs, and leading consumer goods companies that focuses on getting people to wash their hands to avoid the spread of disease. The partnership works to promote and sustain behavior change through a variety of mechanisms, including introducing hygiene practices into school curricula and getting restaurants, clinics, and hospitals to mandate handwashing among employees. Of course, the changed behavior will benefit the business partners by encouraging the purchase of more soap products for handwashing, as well as producing the social benefit of improved public health. Well-designed, culturally and politically sensitive plans for communications and policy change promotion are necessary when you seek to create behavior change at the individual level.

Why Partnerships Fail

Not every partnership succeeds. Despite the best efforts of partners, some partnerships fail to live up to their goals. Most often, partnerships fail for one of two reasons: the wrong solution or the wrong partners.

The wrong solution. PlayPumps International is the cautionary tale of a partnership whose solution went terribly wrong. Much of Africa lacks access to clean water, especially in rural communities. As a result, villagers, usually women, have to spend several hours a day gathering water for home and agricultural use. PlayPumps International sought to address this problem through toy roundabouts (child-powered merry-go-rounds) that would also serve as water pumps. The idea was quite novel—to use children's play to provide the power to pump water for poor communities.

PlayPumps was launched with much fanfare in 2005 by an amazing array of partners, including the Bush administration, the Clinton Foundation, the Case Foundation (founded by AOL's Steve Case), Save the Children, and hip-hop artist Jay-Z. But problems started almost immediately. First, it turned out that the pumps were not terribly effective at delivering water. A study determined that children would have to play on the pump some 27 hours per day to sustain a community. (Of course, this is impossible, since a full day lasts only 24 hours.) Second, the Play-Pumps were expensive—$14,000 each, several times the cost of a conventional hand pump. Third, the wells needed to be sited where there is water, which is not necessarily where children want to play, meaning that local women ended up operating the merry-go-rounds manually. Finally, the pumps proved difficult to maintain, with many being out of commission for a year at a time.

Outside observers began to ask hard questions. The government of Mozambique launched an investigation, which was then picked up by the media, including *The Guardian* newspaper and PBS's *Frontline*. Dismissing these warning signs, the partners pressed ahead, deploying PlayPumps in villages across Africa. In

2010, the partnership finally collapsed, and PlayPumps International closed—a complete failure, leaving more than 1,000 pumps abandoned in villages across Africa.

The PlayPumps saga has many valuable lessons, but among the most important is the fact that the partners were slow to acknowledge that their solution was ineffective. A well-designed partnership with a strong measuring and learning component should enable partners to determine quickly whether their solution is working. If not, it is time to pivot or close down.

The wrong partners. Sometimes a partnership fails because the partners simply cannot work together. Perhaps differences of vision or culture are simply too great; perhaps priorities have changed for one or more of the partners; perhaps the people involved simply can't get along.

An agribusiness partnership brought together an impressive array of partners, including leading donor agencies, foundations, international agricultural research institutions, and leading companies from the seed industry. The goal was to improve agricultural yields by increasing the availability of high-quality seed to smallholder farmers across the two dozen countries of West Africa.

But what started as a promising and potentially impactful partnership fell apart in acrimony for two primary reasons. First, there was a fundamental and insurmountable difference in vision between those partners who favored the use of genetically modified organisms and those who were dead set against their use. Second, some of the personalities involved simply could not work together, and the partner organizations refused to make staffing changes until it was too late. The partnership collapsed, having achieved little.

If you have done a good job of identifying and engaging partners early on, you should be able to uncover such foundational issues before you get into a partnership in the first place. But if priorities or personalities change, it's important to recognize the problem and take steps to address it before it deals a fatal blow to the partnership.

Exiting a Partnership Responsibly

Whether a partnership is successful or not, there usually comes a time when partners begin to think about exiting. There are many possible reasons: shifting business priorities, budgetary cutbacks, personnel changes, evolving market conditions. Whatever your reason for exiting a partnership, there are a few key principles you should abide by.

First, do no harm to your fellow partners or stakeholders. Before you leave the partnership, consider the potential impact on each of your fellow partners and stakeholders. Will your exit doom the partnership to an early demise? Will some of the people you've worked with lose their jobs or their livelihoods? Will beneficiaries of the partnership be left high and dry without resources they were counting on? If problems like these may be caused by your department, look for steps you can take to eliminate or at least mitigate the damage.

Be transparent about your reasons for exiting. Explain your reasons for exiting the partnership as fully and honestly as possible to your partners and stakeholders. This doesn't mean you need to issue a press release or broadcast your reasons via social media. It does mean telling your partners and key stakeholders directly about your departure and its causes. If you skip this step, rumors will fill the void, sometimes causing more damage to the partnership than the simple truth would have caused.

Look for a graceful off-ramp. When insurance company Bima decided to exit the Ghana Fishers Future Partnership, it did so in a gradual way that allowed the remaining partners to plug the gap left by their departure. If your company is exiting a partnership, can you create an off-ramp that leaves time for the remaining partners to find new partners or resources to fill the role your organization played?

Try to fail forward. Failure is painful, but it can also be a powerful learning tool. In Silicon Valley, a failed startup on a professional's resume is viewed as a mark of experience and maturation, and many failed founders have gone on to launch successful new companies. If your partnership does not work out, try to distill the learnings from it and share them with others if possible. After the PlayPumps debacle, the Case Foundation examined what went wrong and shared the key lessons publicly. This isn't an easy thing for any organization to do, but it can help you and others to avoid repeating the same mistakes.

Tie off loose ends. When exiting a partnership, make it a clean break by preparing final reports, archiving data, passing along contact information, and so on. Review the partnership agreement and make sure you've done all you can to live up to your obligations, even if they are not legally binding. If you or your partners have inadvertently created a mess, do all you can to help with the clean up.

The way you exit a partnership, whether it's a success or a failure, speaks volumes about your integrity and that of your company.

To Scale, Sustain, or Exit?

As of early 2020, it's too early to know whether Terry Amartei and the FFP partners in Ghana will be successful in transitioning their partnership from a pilot project to national scale. What's clear, however, is that they are asking the right questions and taking a thoughtful approach to scaling. What's more, FFP has clearly inspired passion among the partners as well as among those they serve. "When I visit a community in Ghana," Terry says, "and I meet with a customer who tells me how our product helped him through a difficult time, that's the kind of experience that drives me."

The decision to scale, sustain, or exit a cross-sector partnership is often a difficult one. Because partnerships take so much time and commitment, it can be very hard to let go. But if you take a thoughtful approach and ask the hard questions that need to be asked, you'll be better positioned to make the decision that is best for your organization, your partners, and your stakeholders.

11

The Essentials
of an Effective
Partnership Team

- Three attributes of effective cross-sector partnership professionals
- Five essential roles in successful partnership teams—and a possible sixth role
- Fostering a culture of collaboration

So far in this book, we've explained why partnerships are important, we've explored their structure, and we've examined how they are built and managed. In this final chapter, we'll turn to the most critical ingredient in a strong partnership: people.

The notion that people make partnerships work may seem obvious, yet the human factor in partnerships is often overlooked. Professionals are thrown into a partnership by circumstance: They happen to work in a business unit looking to partner, they live in a country where a CEO wants to build a partnership, or they have subject-matter expertise in a problem that a partnership is tackling. They may or may not have the personal attributes and skills needed for partnership building. But all too often, a promising partnership fails to take off because key individuals lack those attributes and skills.

So what are the attributes needed to become a partnership pro?

Some may think you need to be a good schmoozer—an extrovert who can cozy up to potential partners at conferences or at cocktail parties. Others may assume you need to be connected—that you need to know the "right people" to be able to forge a partnership.

Neither of these beliefs is correct. Schmoozing and connections may open some doors, but opening doors is just a starting point for building and implementing successful partnerships.

Think about the remarkable business professionals whom we've seen tackling complicated and wicked 21st century business problems in the previous ten chapters of this book. They work for a wide range of companies, large and small, filling a variety of roles from the C-suite to the departments of sustainability, new market development, and corporate affairs. But they all share four attributes that give them an edge in building and managing partnerships.

- ○ *Empathy.* A strong partnership requires a deep understanding and appreciation of the goals, ambitions, worries, interests, fears, and dreams of your partners. Partnership pros are curious about how people from other sectors and industries operate and look at the world. They recognize and respect differences in approach and values across different organizations with different missions and cultures. And, as PepsiCo's Margaret Henry emphasizes, they have "the capacity to listen"—a skill that too often goes underappreciated in the business world.
- ○ *Authenticity.* Just as empathy enables you to understand others, authenticity enables others to understand you and the organizational realities that you need to contend with. Partnership pros are able to share the challenges they face. They speak openly and honestly about their limitations and those of their organizations. They are also frank in the feedback they provide to partners, not for the sake of being critical, but in order to support their partners' growth.
- ○ *Comfort with ambiguity.* A partnership is inherently iterative and changing. As partners discover more about each other and about what they can achieve together, partnerships naturally evolve in scope and focus. A partnership pro is comfortable with the ambiguity and uncertainty that results, and is able to help others become comfortable with them as well—both traits that are rarely seen or rewarded inside large organizations.

○ *Contextual intelligence.* Partnership pros must be able to see situations in the broadest possible context, recognizing differences in values, language, assumptions, and goals and translating them so that partners can find common ground and work together effectively. They can articulate business challenges and opportunities in ways that enable professionals from donor agencies, civil society organizations, government departments, and others to see value for themselves in cross-sector collaboration.

Notice that none of the above attributes requires being an extrovert; they are just as likely to be found in people who consider themselves introverts. Nor do they require any previous network of connections inside or outside the business world. Most important, none of these traits are necessarily innate. They can all be developed and honed with practice.

In my case, I happen to struggle with empathy; it's sometimes hard for me to make a connection with the emotions someone else is feeling. I am working on becoming more empathetic by practicing my listening skills, remembering to acknowledge people's feelings, and recognizing and admitting my biases. By being intentional about honing these attributes, I hope to grow as a partnership professional. For leaders like me, talking about these traits and sharing our own efforts to improve them is one way to develop partnership professionals within our organizations.

The Five Essential Roles in Successful Partnership Teams

While individual attributes are critically important to successful cross-sector partnerships, no single person can carry the weight of building and managing a partnership. A team of dedicated professionals is required. And just as a basketball team generally has players who can fill five distinct roles—the center, the point guard, the shooting guard, and so on—there are five roles that need to be filled in building an effective partnership. The five roles can be played in various ways; you may have some individuals playing multiple roles, and the role played by any one professional may differ from time to time. The main thing is to make sure that someone on your team has responsibility for playing each of the five roles. The roles are:

The networker. Because partnerships begin with connections that lead to opportunities to collaborate, a partnership team needs a strong networker to drive the development of new relationships. An effective networker:

- Knows how to prioritize. Establishing relationships takes time. A good networker can recognize high-potential contacts and takes the time needed to cultivate them.
- Pays it forward. A smart networker knows that life is long, and that being helpful to other people in small ways leaves a positive impression that can produce benefits down the line. Thus, a skilled networker "pays it forward" even in cases where a new contact may not seem likely to be immediately useful—offering a useful referral, sharing an interesting article.

o Never dismisses anyone as unimportant. The skilled networker treats everyone with respect, knowing that it's impossible to predict where they may end up. Five years from today, the intern you just ignored at a conference may be running the country's hottest startup or managing a foundation program with millions of dollars in funding.

o Follows up and follows through. Effective networkers keep their promises. If they told someone they would be in touch, they send the email or make the phone call.

The champion. A partnership team needs someone to provide the energy, political will, and determination to carry the partnership forward from idea to execution. Typically, the champion has some level of status that they can leverage to help push the partnership's needs through the organizational processes and to ensure that the partnership is visible, inside the organization and out. For example, Pearson's Amanda Gardiner was able to engage the head of Pearson's growth markets division, a very respected and influential voice inside the company, as a champion for the partnership with Save the Children (UK). A good champion:

o Invests their personal political capital in the success of a partnership.

o Creates space and time for the partnerships to be incubated and nurtured.

o Secures resources for the partnership—money, staff time, in-kind support, and so on.

○ Communicates within the organization to ensure proper internal alignment.

○ Helps overcome roadblocks, both internal and external, to building and implementing the partnership.

○ Celebrates partnership achievements internally and externally, making sure the team gets the visibility and credit it deserves.

The project manager. At the end of the day, a partnership is about getting things done. So every partnership team needs someone to ensure that things are moving forward on schedule, in scope, and within budget. An effective project manager:

○ Works with partners to define a management plan for partnership activities.

○ Works with partners to establish key measurements regarding business, social, and environmental goals.

○ Aligns resources—budget, staff time, and so on—to ensure timely completion of activities.

○ Tracks the completion of tasks and reports to partners regularly on their status.

○ Works collaboratively with partners to overcome roadblocks and develop solutions to problems.

The organizational sage. As we've seen, internal alignment is critical to the success of a cross-sector partnership. That means you need someone with in-depth knowledge of your organization—its culture, its processes, its history, its values, and its key influencers. A strong organizational sage:

- o Maps out internal structures and processes for moving the partnership forward.
- o Helps identify the right business measurements to ensure the partnership will be valued by internal stakeholders.
- o Helps engage internal stakeholders to ensure buy-in and alignment.
- o Troubleshoots when a partnership encounters an internal roadblock.
- o Helps external partners understand internal processes and culture that may influence the implementation of the partnership.

Relationship manager. Because relationships are the glue that holds cross-sector partnerships together, partnership teams must continually invest in and renew relationships to build trust and transparency. A gifted relationship manager:

- o Fosters effective communication across and among partners.
- o Develops and demonstrates empathy for partners.
- o Builds a deep understanding of partner organization culture and structure.
- o Ensures prompt responses to partner queries and concerns.

PepsiCo's Margaret Henry points out the value of having team members who can serve as "translators" for partners, finding the right language to explain important concepts in terms that are understandable to people from different sectors and cultures. "It is art, not science," Margaret says—a truth that makes the talented translator even more rare and precious.

The Donor Navigator—A Sixth Essential Role

Engaging with large donor agencies—USAID, the World Bank, UN agencies—poses an additional challenge for business professionals: How do you navigate complex, opaque, and sometimes byzantine bureaucracies to make things happen?

If you are working with one of these agencies, you may need a sixth essential role player on your management team—the donor navigator. This is a person who understands how a particular donor agency operates, its culture and structure, and whom to ask when new or tricky questions arise. The donor navigator can also help to translate "development-speak" in the language of business.

Rob Meyers of PepsiCo speaks about the value of the donor navigator: "We identified early on that we needed someone on our team who understand how donors work. This is a skill set you don't find often inside a company." As Rob's comment suggests, your donor navigator may be someone inside your organization or someone from outside with deep institutional knowledge.

Towards a Corporate Culture of Collaboration

A few forward-leaning companies are going further than building partnership teams. They are actually trying to embed the partnership mindset in the entire company.

One leading global consumer goods company, which has been at the forefront of the business sustainability and cross-sector partnership movements, is now in the process of launching a partnership skills training program. The program will help employees across business and functional units to identify, build, and manage cross-sector partnerships. The company's sustainability director says, "We want to give the salesperson in Nigeria and our R&D scientists in Bangladesh the capacity to build and manage these types of partnerships successfully."

As companies are increasingly using cross-sector partnerships to solve complicated and wicked problems, senior leaders must look for opportunities to evolve their corporate cultures, processes, and systems to make collaboration a core element of how they do business. Specifically, businesses need to consider how the following aspects of their managerial systems may impact their ability to engage in cross-sector collaboration.

- *Leadership.* Leaders at all levels of a company need to be able to articulate how cross-sector partnerships can contribute to the company's purpose as well as advancing its business objectives. They also need to work with teams and other leaders in the company to ensure that cross-sector partnerships build value for the business while generating positive social and environmental impacts.
- *Decision-making processes and systems.* Working across sectors on complicated and wicked problems necessarily involves a significant degree of uncertainty and ambiguity, which are hard for many companies to embrace. To deal with these challenges, leaders should look for opportunities to embed iteration, adaptation,

and flexibility into their decision-making processes and management systems, both in the context of partnerships and within broader company processes.

○ *Incentives.* As we've seen, cross-sector partnerships often require the active involvement of many business departments—sustainability, marketing, supply chain, finance, and so on. Incentive structures skewed overwhelmingly towards delivering quarterly results can make it difficult to tackle the longer-term challenges that cross-sector partnerships are best at addressing. In response, business unit leaders need to adopt incentives that look beyond quarterly earnings so that executives and managers can engage on issues that may be crucial for the company's future success.

Building a culture of cross-sector collaboration is not easy. It requires challenging the strictures of 20th century business—siloed management systems, hierarchical leadership structures, a focus on certainty in outcomes—that still pervade most organizations. Companies that can move beyond these traditional business norms will be better equipped to tackle the wicked business problems of the 21st century.

Conclusion

This book began with a description of how a wicked business problem of the 21st century has interwoven the fate of the CEO of a Fortune 500 company, PepsiCo, and that of smallholder farmers in the company's supply chain in India and elsewhere. Over the past several years, Margaret Henry, Rob Meyers, and the Sustainable Agriculture team at PepsiCo have forged a number of partnerships with the UN, NGOs, and other organizations to address their supply-chain challenges. As of this writing (December, 2019), the company is on the cusp on announcing a multimillion-dollar global partnership to enhance the role of women in its agricultural supply chains with the goal increasing the quantity and quality of production in several developing countries. This could be a true game changer, transforming how one of the largest buyers of agricultural commodities in the world engages with and improves the lives of farmers who sell to it and the communities they live in.

Throughout this book, we've seen leading professionals tackling complicated and wicked business problems. We've seen how challenging it can be to build and manage effective cross-sector partnerships to address those problems can be. We've seen how, despite these challenges, cross-sector partnerships enable companies to tackle problems that they could never handle on their own, creating value for business, government, and society through intentional, well-designed collaboration. We've also seen how companies ranging from global players like Medtronic to emerging market champions like miLife in Ghana are using cross-sector partnerships to pilot and scale innovative new business models that deliver results for their businesses while driving lasting social and environmental benefits.

On a personal note, I'm struck by how often these partnerships result in lifelong friendships. Over the course of my career and in the process of researching this book, I've seen many professionals from different sectors and different cultures forge lasting bonds through the process of building and managing a cross-sector partnership. Because partnerships rely on trust, empathy, authenticity, and mutual respect, they make fertile ground for lasting friendships.

As we enter the third decade of the 21st century, the challenges facing the world grow ever more pressing. Meeting and overcoming these challenges is an all-hands-on-deck exercise. Business, civil society, government, academia, and communities must work together effectively if we are to tackle climate change, poverty, inequality, disease, injustice, and the other ills that threaten humankind. Cross-sector partnerships are no panacea, but they can be a powerful tool in our collective toolbox as we address the challenges that lie ahead of us.

I hope this book has provided some tips, tools, and insights that you can use to create value and help address the wicked problems facing our world.

Acknowledgements

I am wonderfully blessed to have had some early mentors and supporters who helped set me forth on my journey. Gabe Hutter, Marsha McGraw-Olive, and the late Bill Maynes and Nelson Ledsky gave me opportunities when I was an eager and earnest but entirely unproven young man. Later, as I was setting out to launch a company, Carol Peasley, Jim Thompson, Terry Myers, Darrell Owen, Paula Goddard, Jerry O'Brien, and Ed Verona were all early believers in my work and vision around cross-sector collaboration.

I am indebted to all the professionals around the world who jumped on Skype calls at odd hours of the day and night to talk to me about their experiences with partnerships. Their stories, insights, and experiences form the heart of this book. Specifically, I want to thank Simon Lowden, Margaret Henry, Rob Meyers, Darian McBain, Chemu Lang'at, Ed Verona, Terry Amartei, Amanda Gardiner, Dondi Mapa, Jaime Arteaga, Ed Martin, Amanda Judge, and David McGinty.

The team at Resonance helped me with this authorship project in a myriad of ways. Zoraya Hightower and Rachel Mullis served as sounding boards and coordinators. Kimberly Davies Lohman made some critical early connections to publishing resources and provided great insights into the process. Dylan Orechovesky helped compile quotes and references for review. Brooke Bauer used her keen eye to sharpen the book's graphics and its cover design. Kristen Sample, Stephanie Landers Silva, Ben Amick, Brenna McKay, Katelin Kennedy, Justin Lawrence,

Shannon Gaffney, Steve Pelliccia, Tait Wardlaw, Lawrence Ang, Seth Olson, Elina Sarkisova, Cara Thanassi, Brett Johnson, James Bernard, and Tess Zakaras all provided invaluable feedback on key concepts and other elements of the book. And through it all, Naa Aku Viens and Angie Gamache helped keep the trains running on time. Without the support of this amazing team of Resonators, this book would not have been possible.

Mary Margaret Frank and Neil Britto were early thought partners on the idea of this book. I am very grateful for their willingness to bounce around ideas about what a book on cross-sector partnerships could look like. My lifelong friend, Danielle Service, provided invaluable feedback on early draft chapters and encouragement.

I want to thank Karl Weber, my editor at Rivertowns Books, for his patient work and remarkable enthusiasm throughout this project. From the first day, he gave very useful advice and feedback. Having worked with some amazing writers and visionaries, Karl had no need to work with a neophyte writer like me. It was a real joy to have Karl shape and improve the writing and flow of the book.

Finally, I want to thank my wife and business partner, Nazgul Abdrazakova. She encouraged me to write this book from the very beginning, and provided tireless moral support and feedback on key ideas.

Steve Schmida
Burlington, Vermont
January, 2020

Appendix A: Sustainable Fisheries Management Project Concept Paper

Background*

While the Government of Ghana recognizes the importance of extending life and vessel insurance to the country's fishermen, Ghana currently lacks a customized, comprehensive insurance package for the fishing sector. Local insurance companies typically view the artisanal fishing sector as too unstructured and thus unattractive for investment. Without insurance for themselves, their crew and their equipment, fishermen are vulnerable to the effects of accidents, illness, and unanticipated natural disasters and shocks, and they lack a pension plan for retirement.

A partnership between SFMP and Millennium Insurance would provide life and vessel insurance for fishermen and their fishing equipment to advance Government of Ghana policy efforts to support the fishing sector. Millennium Insurance is a relatively young insurance company, and it is eager to tap a new

---

* This concept paper, together with supporting data, is available on the USAID website at: https://ghanalinks.org/documents/20181/0/Millennium+Insurance+Strategic+Partnership+Concept+Paper/7588ab55-edc7-440d-bd1f-47256770129e

market for its products by extending insurance to the fishing sector. A partnership with Millennium has the potential to reduce the burden on the Government of Ghana to provide insurance to the sector, and it will provide financial security and improved access to health services for fishermen and their families.

Elsewhere, insurance for the fishing sector is a serious policy initiative. In the Philippines, the Bureau for Fisheries and Aquatic Resources (BFAR) provides a free insurance (life and non-life) package for fishermen. The initiative serves as an incentive for fishermen to register their vessels with the government, providing valuable data for the government to develop policies for the sector.

This concept note outlines a proposed partnership to pilot an insurance program for artisanal fishermen and their equipment in the Central and Western regions of Ghana. As in the Philippines, this insurance program would be linked to registration of canoes and vessels.

Partnership Strategy

The partnership between Millennium Insurance, the Ghana Sustainable Fisheries Management Project (SFMP), and the Government of Ghana would pilot an insurance program tailored to fishermen in Ghana's Central and Western regions.

The key actors for the partnership would be the Ministry of Fisheries and Aquaculture Development (MOFAD), the Fisheries Commission (FC), the National Insurance Commission (NIC), Fishermen Associations and Millennium Insurance. The USAID/ Ghana SFMP would play a central, coordinating role for the partnership.

Millennium Insurance would design the insurance package and provide insurance under the pilot program. It would design its insurance offering with the input of local Fishermen Associations—representing the key beneficiaries for the partnership—and the guidance of the NIC, which regulates the insurance industry in Ghana.

The pilot insurance program could be bundled with the pending SFMP-Vodafone Farmers' Club partnership to deploy Vodafone Cash (or mobile money) for insurance premiums. In the short term, the partners could encourage all fishermen who are members of the Vodafone Farmers' Club to also enroll in the insurance package. The payment for the insurance premiums could then be done via mobile phone through Vodafone Cash. In the medium- to long-term, insurance could be a prerequisite for enrolling in the Vodafone Farmers' Club, with premium payments handled via Vodafone Cash.

Successful implementation of the partnership will require a comprehensive community outreach campaign, to explain the insurance program to fishermen and to tailor it to their needs. The partners (SFMP and MOFAD/FC) will also need to work closely with Millennium to establish a premium rate that will be attractive to the fishermen while also profitable to the company.

Further, Government of Ghana leadership will be crucial to the success of the partnership. MOFAD and FC will be key partners, ensuring that the partnership is in line with and supported by government policy agendas. MOFAD and FC will be closely engaged in each stage of the pilot's design and implementation. MOFAD and FC will be critical to providing Millennium Insurance with baseline data on the fishing sector in Ghana (e.g., number of fishermen, number of canoes, average age, geographical distribution, etc.), needed to support insurance design. Also, to the extent that the insurance pilot may be linked to vessel registration, FC and MOFAD will be responsible for hosting and maintaining the registration system.

Partnership Objectives

- o To increase the security and resiliency of fishermen, by providing life insurance, health insurance, and a pension for retirement.
- o To reduce the need for government expenditure on the fishing sector in times of disaster and unforeseen shocks.
- o To provide financial security to fishermen in the event of the destruction of their vessels or other key equipment, linked to accidents and natural disasters.
- o To reduce dependence on the sea by encouraging voluntary retirement of aged fishermen via a pension scheme.

PROPOSED ROLES AND RESPONSIBILITIES OF PARTNERS

USAID/SFMP Project

1. Collate fishing sector data to inform the development of the insurance package.

2. Undertake monitoring and evaluation of pilot progress and accomplishments based on agreed indicators and deliverables.

3. Lead community sensitization and awareness building to inform the creation of the insurance package and encourage enrollment of fishermen.

3. Serve as partnership secretariat.

Millennium Insurance

1. Outline insurance package–eligible equipment, premiums, claims, etc.

2. Refine insurance package with input of government partners and Fishermen Associations.

3. Recruit and train insurance sales agents/personnel.

4. Open office outlets to bring insurance offerings closer to key fishing communities.

5. Conduct community sensitization and awareness.

6. Undertake monitoring and evaluation of pilot progress and accomplishments based on agreed indicators and deliverables.

MOFAD/FC

1. Provide Millennium with available data on the fishing sector—number of canoes, contact information, age of fishermen, geographic distribution, etc.

2. Provide input into the design of the insurance package.

3. Assist in community sensitization and awareness building for enrollment.

4. If linked with insurance, host and maintain vessel/equipment registration system.

5. Initiate policies to sustain the partnership (e.g. repurposing all or some of the funds meant for the fuel subsidy to subsidize insurance premiums for fishermen).

PROPOSED PHASES OF WORK

Phase 1: Stakeholder Consultations (October-December 2015)

Consultation activities include:

o   Government discussions—gathering input and securing early buy-in from FC and MOFAD.

o   Chief fishermen discussions—gathering input and securing early buy- in from target beneficiaries.

o   Informing National Insurance Commission (NIC) on insurance product—solicit concerns and advice.

o   Refining concept note.

Phase 2: Strategic Partnership Forum (January 2016)

Forum activities include:

o   Presentation of outline for insurance package—premium (life and non-life), claims, eligible fishing equipment, etc.

o   Presentation and discussion of stakeholders' concerns and inputs.

o   Discussion of resources and partnership implementation—exploring and outlining what each partner will contribute.

o   Exploring and discussing strategy to link canoe/vessel registration to insurance scheme for fishermen who have yet to register their canoes with MOFAD/FC.

o   Exploring possible links with the Vodafone Farmers' Club partnership (e.g., Vodafone Cash).

o   Discussing the feasibility of shifting some or the entire current fuel subsidy to an insurance subsidy, to reduce the premium to be paid by fishermen.

o   Refining concept note accordingly.

Phase 3: Pre-Implementation of Partnership (january-May 2016)

Pre-implementation activities include:

o   Finalizing and circulating concept note.

o   Follow-up on outstanding issues from partnership forum.

o   Negotiating partnership and insurance design elements (premium levels, resources from each partner, eligible claims, eligible equipment, etc.).

o   Developing partnership indicators and deliverables.

o   MOU development and signing.

o   Registering insurance product with NIC.

o   Sourcing fisheries sector data from FC and other stakeholders.

o   Sensitization and awareness creation in fishing communities.

o   Selecting appropriate communities for piloting the insur-
ance/registration scheme.

o   Establishing insurance outlets in selected pilot communities.

o   Recruiting and training insurance sales personnel.

Phase 4: Pilot Implementation (May-December 2016)

Implementation activities include:

o   Piloting insurance product, and experimenting with com-
bining insurance product with vessel registration or Vodafone Cash.

o   Sensitization and awareness creation in target communities.

o   Expansion of Millennium office outlets.

o   Monitoring and evaluation – recording outcomes, drawing
lessons learned and refining pilot model.

o   Continuously informing government of partnership outcomes to aid in policy decision-making.

Phase 5: Partnership Scale-Up (January-December 2017)

Partnership scale-up activities include:

o   Extending insurance services to other communities.

o   Opening new Millennium Insurance outlets near fishing
communities.

- o Expanded sensitization and awareness creation.
- o Monitoring and Evaluation – review partnership approaches, add new modalities where necessary, etc.

Phase 6: Partnership Transfer (January-September 2018)

Partnership transfer activities include:

- o Design partnership management modalities and strategies with Millennium, SFMP and MOFAD/FC.
- o Work with Millennium and MOFAD/FC to gradually hand over responsibility for SSG's partnership management tasks to ensure sustainability.

Proposed M&E Outline

Success indicators will include the following:

- o Increase in registration of fishermen, vessels/canoes, gears and other vital equipment.
- o Improved fishing practices and use of approved and recommended fishing equipment.
- o Decrease in the number of fishermen at sea (reduction in fishing effort)—voluntary retirement of aged fishermen.
- o Expanded insurance coverage for fishermen: Enrollment targets met.
- o Customer satisfaction with insurance products.
- o Over time, greater economic security for fishermen and fishing communities; greater resiliency to natural shocks.

Appendix B: Sample Partnership Scorecard

The sample scorecard that follows is based on the original FFP Partnership Concept Note (see Appendix A). It does not necessarily reflect actual FFP partner activities, performance, or timelines. In addition, we've simplified the scorecard contents to make the sample scorecard easier to understand.

The website www.SteveSchmida.com features a downloadable template you can use to develop a customized scorecard for a partnership of your own.

Instructions for Scorecard Use

o The partnership secretariat should develop scorecard tool based on a partnership activity plan developed with input from all partners.

o The partnership secretariat should update the scorecard monthly, tracking rough percentage progress against initial targets, and send it to all partners.

o The partnership secretariat should add new tasks and subtasks to the scorecard as they emerge, or on a monthly basis. Include notes for changed or cancelled activities.

o Partners should review the scorecard quarterly and revise the overall plan as needed.

Sample Partnership Scorecard

Objectives	Tasks	Target Deadline	Sept	Oct	Nov	Dec	Lead Partner	Support Partner
					2016			
Marketing: Growing customer awareness of FFP brand through communications and awareness raising	Focus discussions with chief fishermen and fish processor leaders in Site 1,2,3	Sept 2016	100%				Partner A	
	Finalize design of communications/ marketing plan	Oct 2016	33%	75%	100%		Partner A	Partners B+C+D
	Design communication materials	Oct 2016		33%	75%	100%	Partner A	Partners B+C+D
	Procure communication materials	Nov 2016			Delayed	Delayed	Partner B	

Objectives	Tasks	Target Deadline	Sept	Oct	Nov	Dec	Lead Partner	Support Partner
Sales: FFP customer registration steadily increasing in pilot sites	Establish insurance outlets in Site 1,2,3	Nov 2016	33%	33%	75%	100%	Partner B	
	Recruit registration personnel – Site 1,2,3	Nov 2016		33%	75%	100%	Partner B	Partner D
	Train registration personnel on the product vis-à-vis mobile money	Dec 2016			Delayed	75%	Partner B	Partner D
Continuous Improvement: Performance of platform, product, and outreach monitored to improve FFP design & delivery	Monthly monitoring of registration and claims following FFP launch	Dec 2016 – May 2017				Delayed	Partner B	Partner D
	Pilot Customer Focus Group Study Designed	Feb 2017					Partner A	Partners B+C+D
	FFP Partner Lessons Learned and Design session conducted, to review FFP pilot outcomes and incorporate lessons learned	May 2017					Partner A	Partners B+C+D

Source Notes

Page 5, *There is no recipe:* "What's a Wicked Problem?" Environmental Humanities Working Group, Stony Brook University, https://www.stonybrook.edu/commcms/wicked-problem/about/What-is-a-wicked-problem

Page 7, *Customers want to know:* "Generation Z Believes in Its Own Power to Make Change, But That Companies Must Lead the Way," Sustainable Brands website, October 23, 2019, https://sustainablebrands.com/read/marketing-and-comms/gen-z-believes-in-its-own-power-to-make-change-but-that-companies-must-lead-the-way

Page 7, *according to a 2017 study:* Robert G. Eccles and Svetlano Klimenko, "The Investor Revolution," *Harvard Business Review,* May-June, 2019, https://hbr.org/2019/05/the-investor-revolution

Page 7, *For example, a 2019 study:* Thomas W. Malnight, Ivy Buche, and Charles Dhanaraj, "Put Purpose at the Core of Your Strategy," *Harvard Business Review,* September-October, 2019, https://hbr.org/2019/09/put-purpose-at-the-core-of-your-strategy

Page 8, *Larry Fink, the CEO of BlackRock, Inc.:* Andrew Ross Sorkin, "BlackRock CEO Larry Fink: Climate Change Will Reshape Finance," *New York Times,* January 14, 2020, https://www.nytimes.com/2020/01/14/business/dealbook/larry-fink-blackrock-climate-change.html?action=click&module=Top%20Stories&pgtype=Homepage

Page 10, *a number of excellent resources and publications:* The Intersector Project website, http://intersector.com/; The Partnering Initiative website, https://thepartneringinitiative.org/; The PPPLab website, https://ppplab.org/

Source Notes

Page 15, *Kazakhstan was ranked one of the most corrupt:* Corruption Perceptions Index 2000, Transparency International, https://www.transparency.org/research/cpi/cpi_2000/0

Page 21, *the partnership between Honda and GM:* Fred Lambert, "GM and Honda Are Partnering to Build Next-Gen Batteries for Electric Vehicles," Electrek, June 7, 2018, https://electrek.co/2018/06/07/gm-honda-partner-next-gen-batteries-electric-vehicles/

Page 21, *the well-known Dulles Toll Road:* "Dulles Greenway, Loudon County, VA," Build America Bureau, U.S. Department of Transportation, September 9, 2014, https://www.transportation.gov/policy-initiatives/build-america/dulles-greenway-loudoun-county-va

Page 22, *"a voluntary collaboration": Social Value Investing: A Management Framework for Effective Partnerships,* Columbia University Press, 2018, pages 73-74.

Page 22, *coined the term shared value:* Michael E. Porter and Mark R. Kramer, "Creating Shared Value," *Harvard Business Review,* January-February, 2011, https://hbr.org/2011/01/the-big-idea-creating-shared-value.

Page 31, *fully 90 percent of commercial fish stocks:* Mukhisa Kituyi and Peter Thomson, "90% of Fish Stocks Are Used Up—Fisheries Subsidies Must Stop Emptying the Ocean," World Economic Forum, July 13, 2018, https://www.weforum.org/agenda/2018/07/fish-stocks-are-used-up-fisheries-subsidies-must-stop/

Page 34, *"the job to be done":* Clayton M. Christenson, Taddy Hall, Karen Dillon, and David S. Duncan, "Know Your Customers' 'Jobs To Be Done,'" *Harvard Business Review,* September, 2016, https://hbr.org/2016/09/know-your-customers-jobs-to-be-done

Page 39, *an unprecedented agreement:* "Thai Union Commits to More Sustainable, Socially-Responsible Seafood," Greenpeace International press release, July 11, 2017, https://www.greenpeace.org/international/press-release/7207/thai-union-commits-to-more-sustainable-socially-responsible-seafood/

Page 43, *aims to redefine growth:* "What is a circular economy?" Ellen MacArthur Foundation website, https://www.ellenmacarthurfoundation.org/circular-economy/concept

Page 44, *a coalition of companies, governments, NGOs, and foundations:* Full disclosure: Resonance is a partner of PACE, and author Steve Schmida serves on the PACE Leadership Group.

Page 46, *"the commitment of a group of actors":* John Kania and Mark Kramer, "Collective Impact," *Stanford Social Innovation Review,* Winter, 2011, https://ssir.org/articles/entry/collective_impact

Page 46, *reducing the volume of plastic:* "About Us," Global Plastic Action Partnership, https://www.weforum.org/gpap/about-us

Page 51, *the Clean Cooking Alliance is dedicated:* "About," The Clean Cooking Alliance, https://www.cleancookingalliance.org/home/index.html

Page 52, *it is critical to have an exit strategy:* "More Than the Sum of Its Parts: Making Multi-Stakeholder Initiatives Work," Global Development Incubator, November 2015, https://globaldevincubator.org/wp-content/uploads/2016/02/Making-MSIs-Work.pdf

Page 54, *There are five essential elements:* "What Is Collective Impact?" Sol Price Center for Social Innovation, University of Southern California, https://socialinnovation.usc.edu/wp-content/uploads/2018/06/Collective-Impact-Handout.pdf

Page 60, *despite the incredible proliferation:* "Global Internet Growth Stalls and Focus Shifts to 'Meaningful Universal Connectivity' to Drive Global Development," Press release, International Telecommunication Union, September 22, 2019, https://www.itu.int/en/mediacentre/Pages/2019-PR16.aspx

Page 74, *According to an independent study:* "Making the Transition from Pilot to Scale: Examining Sustainability and Scalability Issues in a Public-Private Telecenter Partnership in Sri Lanka," by Laura Hosman, *Information Technology for Development,* July, 2011, pages 232-248.

Page 77, *heart disease is responsible:* "Kenya Launches National Cardiovascular Disease Management Guidelines," World Health Organization, https://www.afro.who.int/news/kenya-launches-national-cardiovascular-disease-management-guidelines-0

Page 81, *drilling down below surface phenomena:* Eric Ries, "The Five Whys for Start-Ups," *Harvard Business Review,* April 30, 2010, https://hbr.org/2010/04/the-five-whys-for-startups

Page 117, *Companies that have a well-defined sense of purpose:* Sally Blount and Paul Leinwand, "Why Are We Here?" *Harvard Business Review,* November-December 2019, https://hbr.org/2019/11/why-are-we-here

Page 136, *A powerful tool for helping companies:* "Sustainable Development Goals," United Nations, https://sustainabledevelopment.un.org/sdgs

Page 139, *It has worked with more than 9,000 companies:* United Nations Global Compact website, https://www.unglobalcompact.org

Page 140, *GDA provides resources:* USAID Global Development Alliances website, https://www.usaid.gov/gda

Page 140, *especially Asia and the Pacific:* Business Partnerships Platform website, https://dfat.gov.au/aid/who-we-work-with/private-sector-partnerships/bpp/Pages/business-partnerships-platform.aspx

Page 140, *"support multinational companies":* "Business Partnerships Fund," Business Innovation Facility, UKaid, https://www.bifprogramme.org/where-we-work/business-partnerships-fund

Page 140, *initiated through Sweden's embassies:* "About SIDA," https://www.sida.se/English/

Page 141, *leveraging power dynamics in negotiations:* "Power in Negotiation: How Effective Negotiators Project Power at the Negotiating Table," Harvard Law School Program on Negotiation, December 3, 2019, https://www.pon.harvard.edu/daily/negotiation-skills-daily/enhance-your-negotiating-power/

Page 165, *in-country activists protested:* "We Want Monsanto Out of Nepal: An Interview with an Activist," *Global South Development Magazine,* January, 2012, https://www.gsdmagazine.org/get-monsanto-out-of-nepal-an-interview-with-an-activist/

Page 171, *a technique pioneered by the World Bank:* "Logframe," Better Evaluation website, https://www.betterevaluation.org/en/evaluation-options/logframe/

Page 172, *three development economists won the Nobel Prize:* Jeanna Smialek, "Nobel Economics Prize Goes to Pioneers in Reducing Poverty," *New York Times,* October 14, 2019, https://www.nytimes.com/2019/10/14/business/nobel-economics.html

Page 179, *an extensive and detailed indicator library:* "An Introduction to Impact Measurement and Management," Global Impact Investing Network, https://iris.thegiin.org/introduction/#b3

Page 189, *a small part of Ghana's vast informal economy:* Ariella Cohen, "The 70 Percent in Ghana (Hint: It's the Informal Sector)," The Rockefeller Foundation's Informal City Dialogues, April 9, 2013, https://nextcity.org/informalcity/entry/the-70-percent-in-ghana-hint-its-the-informal-sector

Page 192, *Literally: lightning scaling:* Tess Townsend, "Reid Hoffman: The First Three Stages of Blitzscaling," *Inc.,* November 2, 2015,2015, https://www.inc.com/tess-townsend/reid-hoffman-three-stages-of-blitzscaling.html

Page 193, *a 2014 analysis of cross-sector partnerships:* Larry Cooley and Johannes F. Linn, "Taking Innovations to Scale: Methods, Applications and Lessons," Results for Development Initiative, September, 2014, https://www.usaid.gov/sites/default/files/documents/1865/v5web_R4D_MSI-BrookingsSynthPaper0914-3.pdf

Page 193, *scaling in two dimensions:* Clayton M. Christensen, Efosa Ejomo, and Karen Dillon, "Cracking Frontier Markets," *Harvard Business Review,* January-February, 2019, https://hbr.org/2019/01/cracking-frontier-markets

Page 194, *There are three main options:* "Pathways to Scale: A Guide on Business Models and Partnership Approaches to Scale-Up," USAID, October 17, 2016, https://www.usaid.gov/cii/pathways-scale

Page 198, *results like these would place Topica:* Jon Russell, "Topica Raises $50M for Its Online Learning Services in Southeast Asia," *TechCrunch,* November 27, 2018, https://techcrunch.com/2018/11/27/topica-raises-50m/

Page 198, *50 percent of students:* Topica website, https://topica.asia/

Page 198, *which Tuan has done very successfully:* Author's note: I was unable to interview Tuan for this book. However, I pieced together elements of this story from discussions with Tuan in 2010 as well as subsequent information on Topica's website. My apologies for any errors or omissions.

Page 206, *the Global Handwashing Partnership:* Global Handwashing Partnership website, https://globalhandwashing.org/

Page 207, *the pumps proved difficult to maintain:* Andrew Chambers, "Africa's Not-So-Magic Roundabout," *The Guardian,* November 24, 2009, https://www.theguardian.com/commentisfree/2009/nov/24/africa-charity-water-pumps-roundabouts

Page 207, *the government of Mozambique launched an investigation:* "Troubled Water," *Frontline World,* https://www.pbs.org/frontlineworld/stories/southernafrica904/video_index.html

Page 210, *the Case Foundation examined:* Jean Case, "The Painful Acknowledgment of Coming Up Short," Case Foundation, May 4, 2010, https://casefoundation.org/blog/painful-acknowledgment-coming-short/

Page 215, *Contextual intelligence:* Nick Lovegrove and Matthew Thomas, "Triple-Strength Leadership," *Harvard Business Review,* September, 2013, https://hbr.org/2013/09/triple-strength-leadership

Index

About the Author

Steve Schmida is the Founder and Chief Innovation Officer of Resonance, an award-winning global development and corporate sustainability consulting firm with more than 100 consultants worldwide and offices in Vermont, Washington, D.C., Seattle, and Manila. Resonance clients include Fortune 500 companies, international donor agencies, and leading nonprofits and foundations.

Steve has been at the forefront of corporate sustainability and global development for more than two decades, focusing on developing cross-sector partnerships that enable clients to tackle "wicked problems" from climate change to human trafficking in supply chains. His writing has appeared in the *Huffington Post*, *Stanford Social Innovation Review*, and the *Moscow Times*. He sits on the Leadership Group of the Platform for Accelerating the Circular Economy (PACE) and on the Sustainable Innovation Executive Council of the Grossman School of Business at the University of Vermont.

Prior to founding Resonance, Steve lived and worked for eight years in Russia and Central Asia, where he established and led programs to support entrepreneurs and civic activists for the Eurasia Foundation and the National Democratic Institute. Fluent in Russian, he holds an M.A. from the Fletcher School of Law and Diplomacy at Tufts University. He lives in Vermont with his wife, Nazgul (who is CEO of Resonance), and their two children.